Incidental
Grace

Incidental Grace

ROBERT H. POPE

Zondervan Books
Zondervan Publishing House
Grand Rapids, Michigan

Zondervan Books are published by Zondervan Publishing House, 1415 Lake Drive, S.E., Grand Rapids, Michigan 49506

Incidental Grace
Copyright © 1985 by The Zondervan Corporation
Grand Rapids, Michigan

Library of Congress Cataloging in Publication Data

Pope, Robert H.
   Incidental grace.

   Bibliography: p.
   1. Pope, Robert H. 2. Reformed Church—United States—Cler-gy—Biography. 3. Reformed Church in America—Clergy—Biogra-phy. 4. Christian biography—United States. I. Title.
   BX9543.P67A36   1985   285.7'32'0924 [B]   84-27154
   ISBN 0-310-34651-7

Edited by John Sloan
Designed by Kim Koning

Printed in the United States of America

85   86   87   88   89   90 / 10   9   8   7   6   5   4   3   2   1

Contents

Preface

I'm a two-career man. The first career I chose; the second caught me by surprise. Though I loved the first, now that I've tasted the second, I could never return to where I was. Though the first had the potential of great reward, the second bears a prize I can no longer imagine being without. Though the first was proudly achieved alone, the second led to a blessed apprenticeship that has now appraised the solitary pursuit of the proud to be the lesser life, the poorer life. In the first career, I spent over ten years as a mechanical engineer doing stress analysis and engine design in aircraft- and rocket-engine systems. My last assignment: project engineer on the rocket-descent engines for Surveyor, the first soft-instrument-landing package for the moon. The pages that follow tell about the second career, Minister of the Pascack Reformed Church in Park Ridge, New Jersey, as well as the first.

There would be no story without the second career, nor for that matter, without the first. But what makes the story important is not the dual vocation, not the change in midstream. The importance of the interruption lies with the Intervener . . . the Intruder . . . the Transcendent One. *He* caught me by surprise. *He* led me to a vocation I seemed to have the least qualification for. *He* reordered my values, redefined my understanding of success, and renewed my life with bits and pieces of happiness of incredible consequence.

This book, though autobiographical, is not *autobiography*. It is about God. It is about one soul who encountered the author of all souls; the one who still lives within the episodes of our daily lives, invades us, and changes us against all odds. It is a story of hope, of the power of God, of the green pastures where he leads men and women of faith.

I hope the story will open up possibilities for those who have written off a large part—possibly the most important part—of their lives. It is for the scientific personality; those who through logic, sound judgment, and a courageous adherence to facts have missed "the smell of unseen roses." We often overlook a vast share of life, especially those of us who at some young age sat at the back of a Sunday-school class, arms folded and chairs tipped back, thinking, "Oh, yeah? Prove it to me!"

The story is not intended to inspire more people toward two careers. It offers a second insight to the reader, not a second vocation. The world does not need more preachers, heaven knows! The world needs believing, inspired people in their current roles, making decisions based on the commands of Christ.

My plea to you, the reader, and I hope you will be the skeptic and the pragmatist, is to read with the mind of a scientist, ready to consider the data presented in the story. And just as any worthy theory emerges in science, a new world may emerge that you have yet to discover that contains a haunting joy that you have yet to find.

> "Yet man is born to trouble
> as surely as sparks fly upward."
>
> ————Job 5:7————

1

Born to Lose

Actually, no one wanted to be there. A sense of tragedy, futility, and loss dominated the room. Only the dutiful came—in spite of their increasing pain of grief after each visit. The patient, young at fifty, had been comatose for a month. No one understood why she had taken too many prescription drugs with a martini chaser. Did she do it deliberately? No one knew. Now the brain monitor showed nothing. Yet the breathing continued.

When I had approached her room earlier, a nurse at the door had made sure that visitors wore the masks, gowns, and gloves provided. I had put on a mask, promised not to touch anything, and entered. The machinery, tubes, and heart monitor that were plugged into the patient maintained the life that would have otherwise escaped her. A technician took notes and adjusted the equipment. I didn't say anything. I prayed. I wondered about that bunch of cells that lay in the bed.

Before the tragedy she had everything our world judges a success: a daughter at Princeton; another daughter married to a man in the insurance business; a successful husband who gave her everything she wanted—far beyond any material need. By all outward appearances, she had it made. I wondered what had happened. It didn't matter about the drugs and alcohol— what order she took them in or what her intentions were. What mattered, I thought, was whether she had a chance to avoid this calamity. Had she been programmed to believe that the outward goals were the most important: cleanliness, orderliness, an energetic husband with a good job, a couple of children in good health who didn't cause too much grief, a pair of Eldorados in the garage, a poolside cocktail party—the good life? Did she, or do any of us, have the chance to believe anything else? Do we understand the alternatives to a culture that would entrap, deceive, and defraud us?

Some people say what makes us human is the ability to shape our destinies. Nature has strict intentions for everything else. A bird spends its life foraging for food, building nests, avoiding predators, and singing when it mates. A worm keeps the soil loose and seeks out the richest organic pockets of growth and blackness. A dog has no choice but to be a dog—to make love in heat, bark at the garbage man, lie at the feet of those who give it a little shelter, warmth, and affection. But people are supposed to be different. We have the options of school, vocation, and play; most of us choose whom we will marry, where we will live, how many children we will have, and what kind of car we will drive.

Yet as I looked at the still-tanned remains of free choice, I wondered if she had been programmed like everything else. Would it have taken an exceptional human being to avoid those things that led her to that tragic moment? Was she locked into a dubious formula for happiness? Perhaps our choices are few, whether in a respectable white suburb or a black urban ghetto, unless courage, maturity, exceptional circumstances, or God prevail.

We learn our lessons well. The principles for living are very specific. We understand them to be: too much passion is deadly; life is concrete; business is in our best interest; our home and neighborhood bring credibility; no one will take care of us if we don't take care of ourselves; knowledge is everything provided it's practical; the only thing to fear is failure and bankruptcy; power brings security; bank accounts give us peace; status produces friends; too much religion threatens respectability, but a little religion is good for the kids. We learn these codes of behavior in unspoken ways through our mother's hopes, our father's absences, and our own misconceptions of joy.

As I pondered this tragedy, it made me appreciate how incredible and dramatic the rescue had been in my own life. At one time I, too, had been securely locked into the beliefs that warp our values. Those beliefs keep us isolated from anything that would enlarge our capacity for empathy and generosity. They convince us of the absurdity of God's miraculous grace, and they shrink our joy into small satisfactions from brief pleasures. I, too, had floundered blindly through the early decades of life.

There, among the tubes and plumbing and machinery, I found myself—but for the grace of God.

Some people, however, though generally incapable of it, go against the odds, defy the expected, and surprise us with good. They are people who offer a rare sacrifice without counting the cost; who act honestly without motive; who do deeds of pure mercy; who believe in something when everything seems to confirm unbelief and despair. These are the exceptional people. And I count myself as one. If that sounds egotistical, I mean precisely the opposite.

I escaped that tragic end of medical plumbing because of an incredible mercy in our midst that persuades us, urges us, pleads with us, and begs for our attention and loyalty. Suddenly, in that hospital room, I had an overwhelming sense of humility, a powerful sense of gratitude that God had rescued me from a similar end. I knew I needed to tell of that mercy. I felt compelled to speak of all the joy and trouble, the struggle and yearning, the hope and fulfillment—all the gifts I had been given.

This is a story of escape, a tale of how the exceptional can rise from the mediocre. This is a story about God's mercy. I tell it in praise of God and to his glory.

My parents made it the hard way. My father was raised in the suburbs of Boston. He was one of ten kids living in a homestead that didn't have an indoor toilet until the end of the thirties. He worked his way farther up the ladder of success than any of his siblings. After being crippled in a boyhood accident, he learned to walk with a permanently rigid knee. He rode the trolley to Boston where he studied in one of the night institutes at the Massachusetts Institute of Technology, and during his student years, he often had nothing more than a handful of peanuts for supper. Like his favorite novelist, Horatio Alger, he believed in hard work, honesty, opportunity, and sacrifice. He was totally convinced that in America this formula couldn't fail; generally, for him, it didn't.

He traveled to England and France during World War I as a field representative for Locomobile cars. My mother, narrowly missing passage on the ill-fated Lusitania, followed him, and they married in London during the Zeppelin blitz. Later he became an executive engineer for Raybestos Manhattan and always had work during the depression.

My mother came from similar circumstances. She lived with her parents and her ten brothers and sisters in West Haven, Connecticut. There she learned to deprecate sex, work hard, have faith in God, and devote total attention to the males around her. Her father, whose ancestral line reached back to British loyalists in the colonies, came from Canada where his grandfather had sought refuge from the rebellion. Her father, a carriage maker, watched his trade dwindle with the coming of the motor car. The family struggled, but they kept a sense of humor and knew how to laugh.

I was the second son of parents who had made it by plain living and hard work. I lived in a world where pot roast was the most exciting food on the table. In our family, emotion was an unsightly embarrassment, and conversation was uncolored by feelings or passions. We carefully avoided demonstrative affection, never mentioned love-making, and seldom appreciated joy. Friends were unheard of. The self-made need no support—

friends, God, crutches, and welfare were for the weak, the unworthy, and the lazy. My father hated Roosevelt, the Boston Irish, and anyone who expected something he or she didn't earn. By his own determination he outdistanced the poverty that would have kept him in a Taunton shoe factory. If he could do it, so could anyone else.

My upbringing lead me to value the same conclusions. The goals that were worthiest of us were respectability, courage, self-preservation, honesty, education, work, and money in the bank. We were supposed to believe in the free-enterprise system, opportunity for all, and our own strength. We were taught to distrust anything that was too feminine, sexual, or emotional, and anything that was too religious—Catholics in particular.

As I see it now, I didn't fit the system. I lived through a miserable childhood. To this day I don't know what made it so tough for me. Was it a bunch of genes that stirred that permanent restlessness and discontent within me? Was it some chemistry of the flesh? Or was it a specific incident that I have long forgotten that imbedded itself in my unconscious mind and produced doubt and uncertainty about my personal worth? What subtle series of incidents, words, attitudes, and impressions convinced me that I was less than acceptable? I remember listening without conviction to Bible stories in Sunday school; what squelched my capacity to believe?

Perhaps we lose our ability to believe when we become cynical. I don't know exactly when, but at some tragic moment, I became convinced that life was devoid of pleasure. Even a rare moment of happiness was a negative experience for me, as if it were undeserved, a failure of the intellect, or a wild immorality. I couldn't understand people who found pleasure in simple things like parades, card games, and afternoons at the beach. Perhaps we are like the child who pushes aside the peas on the plate, vows never to eat them, and feeds them one by one to the eager dog under the table. For nearly a lifetime, we believe peas to be the invention of some diabolical creator, and then one day we taste fresh peas from the garden. In one brief, sudden rush of sweet flavor we realize how much we have missed by living in the bland world of frozen dinners. What inner attitudes shaped by a hundred lost perceptions carve out and permanently mold our destiny? What hidden vows do we make to ourselves that we carry with us forever?

And what of God? What is he doing about our misconceptions? How does he lead us to a different end than we suppose awaits us? He opposes sin; therefore, he opposes us as long as we live a lie and take seriously our false beliefs. He is against our twisted images, pettiness, fears, self-doubts, and misconceived notions. And because he is against them, he is forever *for us*. He seeks to speak through all the irritation, storms, blackness, and depression; he is shouting at us, "Take a another look. The reality and the dream are far different than you suppose."

Memories still linger in my consciousness that for years fostered misconceptions about myself.

I recall at an early age (perhaps in kindergarten or first grade) playing on the playground. Although I don't remember why, I found myself in a fight with another boy. We pushed and shoved. I knocked him down, and he cried. Several people grabbed me and told me I would be sent home. I thought I must have hurt him very badly, and fear gripped me so completely that I was never able to hit anyone after that. If I couldn't avoid a fight, I lost. I was paralyzed by the fear that if I asserted myself too aggressively, I might hurt someone and get into trouble.

I have another early memory. I liked to ice-skate and did it well. There was a pond across the street from our house, and in winter I had many opportunities to play hockey. In every other sport I would be the last to be chosen, except in hockey. One time we chose up sides for a game, and a new kid on the block wanted to play. He could hardly manage the skates; his ankles turned over every step he took. After the sides were determined, he alone remained. Enjoying the moment because for once I wasn't the last kid to be picked, I said, "You guys can have him. He's no good." The image of that boy's face has remained with me forever. It was a symbol of my own ability to add pain to someone else's life, and that memory lingered on the fringes of my consciousness for years.

Another memory is clear in my mind. Once several neighborhood kids made a backyard high jump; it even had a pit and a crossbar. Everyone jumped better than I did. Determined to jump higher, I set the bar at the level everyone else had achieved, and after they had gone home I tried until dark to clear it. It became a self-defeating effort—the more I tried, the more tired I became and the less likely I was to succeed. Exhausted, I went home in the dark, a failure.

I became a loner. I enjoyed listening to Beethoven and Brahms. I had a paper route. I took small proud pleasure in walking back up three flights of stairs to return three cents I had shortchanged a customer. World

War II groaned in the background, and even though my grades didn't predict talent, I dreamed of being an airplane designer.

My brother was making it. He went to Yale in New Haven. We lived only twenty-five miles away in Stratford, and occasionally, on Sunday afternoons, we would drive up to see him. Because of my father's lameness and my mother's reluctance, I would be asked to run up the several flights of stairs to his room and tell him we had arrived. I had tremendous admiration for him. He was fulfilling every expectation that our parents had of us. Yale, a prestigious college from which an uncle and a cousin had graduated, seemed to be the epitome of knowledge and achievement. The magnificent gothic buildings nearly breathed dignity, knowledge, pride, honor, and for me, unattainable success. One of my brother's friends, who had often seen me go in and out of the dorm, jokingly asked if I was a child prodigy, a genius. Everybody laughed. But I wished with all my heart that it were so.

As I see it now, God, in his rich mercy, followed me even then. The reason I didn't fit in was God had another plan for me. I failed because a different mission awaited me, one that I would have completely misunderstood if I had known about it then. At times God allowed me to feel the full misery of my guilt so that I might later see in a dramatic way his incredible forgiveness. The God whom Paul described as "rich in mercy ... when we were dead"[1] shaped and molded my life. Though it takes the hindsight of faith to see it, a marvelous landscape lies behind us, filled with the purposes of God the forerunner.

In the book of Exodus, God led the Israelites with a

pillar of cloud by day and a column of fire by night. Some interpreters speculate that this was a distant volcano that smoldered in the day and glowed in the darkness. However we interpret it, God was clearly the one who was leading those men and women as they sought to avoid the Egyptian army. I knew something of that same cloud and fire. But if someone had told me that all the cynical laughter, the mocking, the failure, and the inner pain were actually the cloud and fire of God, I would not have understood them at all.

Yet it's not so incredible, is it, this grace of God that leads us and prepares us? Often we miss God's leading entirely. Later in my ministry, when a beautiful Christian woman died of cancer at thirty-eight, all of us in the church wondered what God had intended. As usual, the realization of how serious her illness was came to us gradually. After the inevitable round of biopsies, the horrifying word "inoperable" penetrated our consciousnesses. The radiation burned into her flesh; the chemotherapy made her hair fall out; her stomach was perpetually nauseated. The sterile hospital world surrounded her at a time when warmth, color, and companionship were needed. We prayed.

We had our first healing service. We spoke tenderly of a loving God. We approached the inevitable with faith. How many hours and days and months of pain would she have before the end came? And we wondered what God was doing. One day as I rode through lower Manhattan, I saw the derelicts, the hopeless souls cast up on the fringes of the city by the waves of human greed and selfishness, and I asked, Why not them Lord? Why such a beautiful soul? And again I wondered what God was doing.

But we had overlooked one fact—God was going ahead, preparing this woman for her supreme moment of hardship. That God had deserted her seemed obvious *unless* we take into account all the years he had spent meticulously and patiently enriching her faith so that she might be able to see through the darkness. Who can say how he did it? Possibly even she couldn't tell us if we had asked her. Perhaps he had shaken the foundations until she found the foothold she needed to sustain her life. Perhaps he had denied her some success, some wealth, to keep her from too much contentment and comfort. Maybe in some marvelous way he had given her the most precious gift—a relentless hunger and thirst for righteousness. Who knows?

In his rich mercy, God had gathered all the ingredients in her life—the laughter, the disappointments, the achievements, the yearnings, the anxieties, the hopes—and through them he touched something within her that grew into the courage and trust and faith she would need to fight her biggest battle. The simple but difficult truth is that God is present in all the events that swirl around us; he sees far better than we what lies ahead. Though often quoted in a glib and careless way, the words of William Cowper's hymn offer us a hope-filled insight:

> God moves in a mysterious way,
>   His wonders to perform;
> He plants his footsteps in the sea,
>   And rides upon the storm.
>
> Deep in unfathomable mines
>   Of never failing skill
> He treasures up his bright designs,
>   And works his sovereign will.

It is not foolish to believe that God is going ahead, preparing us for what is to come. Don't we do the same for our children? Don't we think of the calamities that could befall them and keep the stairs safely closed off and our cabinets cleared of poisons? Don't we foresee the dangers and carefully prepare our children to cope with them? Don't we teach them the hazards of traffic and a fear of the suspicious stranger? Don't we encourage them to learn a trade or occupation to protect them from poverty and hardship? So it is with God. And so he did for me. There he was, planting bench marks, anchors, incidents of grace that I could later look back on and praise him for. At that point, though, I wasn't accepting Christ. I couldn't—I didn't understand enough yet to accept anything.

"In the desert prepare
the way for the LORD;
make straight in the wilderness
a highway for our God."

————ISAIAH 40:3————

2

Moorings Along the Way

My mother took us to church. I first heard about God and Christ from her, and for that I will always be grateful. I also recall finding her on her knees praying out loud, and I was intensely ashamed that she would do such a thing where others in the family could hear her.

I believe one of the most serious obstacles to faith is the feeling that religion is an emotional embarrassment. When the greatly respected nobleman is discovered in bed with the maid, the enlightened people say, "How could he stoop so low and fall for such a common passion?" That is the way many "enlightened" people feel about anyone who embraces religion. Many well-informed people also see religion as the business of those with low intelligence and high emotions. They keep the old Sunday-school picture in their minds of a humorless, stern, insensitive place, run by opinionated old ladies with bun hairdos who are completely empty headed when it comes to practicalities.

These feelings, of course, came from my father. Once when Billy Graham, who was speaking from Madison Square Garden, appeared on the television, my father laughed and said it was just what the city of New York needed. "They tried everything else keeping those ignorant, disorderly people in line; why not Billy Graham!" He boasted that he only went to church once—to fix the clock. I never saw him inside a church in my entire life except on our wedding day.

Religion, like sex, remained unmentionable in our world—no explanations. We simply understood that we should never talk about certain things.

It would be years before I overcame the embarrassment that gripped me when I publicly talked of my faith. The fact is, it took a well-timed funeral to give me enough freedom to declare my faith and destiny to my family.

The church we went to was an old Episcopal Church in Stratford, Connecticut. For me it inspired a strange mixture of fascination and boredom. The liturgical Episcopal worship intrigued me. Probably for the first time in my life, I felt a strange attraction to something important. I remember the poor man who constantly dunned the boys my age to be acolytes or to carry the cross in front and behind the choir. How difficult we made his life. We avoided him, promised to be there and then didn't show up (so long as our mothers didn't know), and made fun of his peculiar gait—he would pitch forward, walking as if he were trying to smell his way along, like a hound dog following a woodchuck.

Secretly I was glad when he asked me to participate in the worship and looked forward to being a part of the ritual. I discovered in the liturgy a haunting sense of warmth and well-being.

One Easter Sunday I carried the cross at the end of the choir procession. The smell of the flowers; the freshly pressed choir and clergy surplices; the intricately carved wood, dark and patinaed by over a century of worshipers; the mystical feeling of being inside the altar screen and therefore, it seemed, closer to God—all these things filled me with a sense of wonder and mystery. Just at that high moment, a crash interrupted my euphoria. The boy who was carrying the lead cross, who was six and a half feet tall and weighed over two hundred and fifty pounds, had fainted. Our hound-dog friend, by some divine gift of strength, pulled him unobtrusively into the sacristy while I wondered in wide-eyed astonishment how anything so disruptive and inconsiderate could happen while we were so close to heaven. In spite of my childishness, I believe these occasions of mystical awe were the first faint beckonings toward a home that I would yet discover as my own.

Sunday school turned me off. All I can remember are the Bible pictures we were given that showed men and women in their bathrobes doing unbelievable things and looking like no one I ever met, with their pallid angelic innocence that spoke of no pain or suffering or struggle. I could hardly wait to grow up so that I could finally announce to my mother that I was not going to church anymore. At seventeen I did just that. And I never returned until I was thirty-five. I had every intention of being just like my father.

He was a good father, and I loved him very much—*idolized* might be a better word. He was highly moral, hard working, faithful to my mother, intensely honest in his business dealings; I cherished every moment he gave us. One time in downtown Bridgeport I was walking back to the car with him, and we discovered a cop writing out a parking summons. How shocked I was that anyone would dare summon my father to anything.

He gave me moorings, too. These gifts included a respect for authority and a desire to search deeper for meanings and truths, and though he had much pride, he also had an immense intellectual humility. I remember coming home from college once with a textbook for a new course in machine design. Since I had worked my way through school as a tool designer and draftsman, I tended to look down my nose at the book. As I tossed it to him, I said, "This is one book I won't have to read!"

As he opened the pages carefully, the crackling of the binding announced the book's lack of use. Peering over his glasses, he responded, "Don't ever think you know everything about anything."

I recall another incident that has stayed with me. When I was very young, he took me to the plant where he worked in the industrial section of Bridgeport. The depressed thirties had reduced the area to pitiful desolation. Litter blew across the streets, propelled by the wind of an especially cold winter. The cheerless, lifeless windows of mills and manufacturing lofts peered over fences along narrow desolate streets. His business lasted an hour or so, and as we got into the car to go home, a young girl appeared who was obviously cold, destitute, and forsaken—clearly a victim of the depression. She approached my father for money. I was too young to evaluate her sincerity, but something in her must have moved him, because he took five dollars out of his pocket and gave it to her. Five dollars was an incredible amount of money to me and to many people then. It represented a week's worth of groceries. I remember how shocked I was. I remember the tears on the face of the young woman. But I especially recall the intense admiration in a little boy's heart for his father as we drove home through the cold, dying streets of Bridgeport.

As I look back on my high-school years, I find them marked by a special lack of color, achievement, and joy; it was just a period in my life I lived through. All along I planned to be an engineer. The only courses I excelled in were chemistry, physics, and mathematics; languages, grammar, spelling, and music were disasters. Having no intense desire to achieve anything else, I opted for what seemed to be my destiny with a quiet, uncomplaining acceptance, not seriously considering any other direction. As I see it now, the emptiness, the lack of conviction, the absence of passion for anything—all prepared me, by grace, for the all-consuming passion.

I remember reading A.J. Cronin's romantic novel *The Citadel* and wishing I had the dedication, conviction, and commitment of the story's hero, Doctor Manson. His life became a relentless battle to see medicine dedicated to the well-being of the patient rather than to the benefits of the physician. I yearned for something to die for since I had not found anything in particular to live for—a situation which would later lead me to understand the paradox of God's presence in his absence. Sometimes, because we are not ready to accept him, he absents himself by grace. This kind of grace protects us from prematurely rejecting him because of our pride—a rejection that we may never be able to reverse. In my case, the gift I received was a mildly disturbing lack of interest in anything. A total dedication to machine design, personal accomplishment, making money, or pleasure might have completely satisfied me and left no emptiness to eventually be filled to overflowing. Thirty years later I had a shocking look at what early dedications and commitments can do to people. It happened when my wife, Joey, and I attended my high-school class reunion.

I had not seen my classmates in thirty years. To refresh my memory beforehand, I dug my yearbook out of a musty box of junk in our cellar and drifted through it, recalling all the familiar or forgotten faces. I wondered about the decades gone by—the births, deaths, disappointments, joys, struggles, circumstances, successes, failures that had occurred to all of us. How would I catch up with it all in one evening?

To my surprise, I quickly discovered that nearly everyone was the same as they were on the day we graduated. Before Joey and I could check our coats, a balding, loudly dressed man grabbed my hand; he was the self-appointed welcoming committee. Startled, I searched his face for some clue to remember him by. Finally, daring to guess, I stammered, "Bill Crawford?" His quick affirmation suddenly brought it all back. I knew exactly who he was; he was an operator way back then. He always knew the system. Like a cat he always managed to land on his feet. He never got a detention. He was perpetually promoting something. He said he now sold soap and household products. He pressed his business card into my hand, promised to look me up, and rushed across the room to greet another newly arrived couple.

Joyce, the first date I ever had (an Irish Catholic, to my father's dismay), appeared. Across the room she looked as I remembered her. She still had that curious posture suggesting an eagerness to hear and accept what was being said. Later, as I got close, I could see the weariness in her face confirming the fact that she had ten kids.

Sam, a successful scientist working on food research, and his wife sat with us. "You're Bob Pope, aren't you?" he inquired as we sat down. "I'm Sam Proctor, and my wife, Kathy."

"Sure, I remember you. How are you?" I said.

"Someone said you're a minister."

"That's right."

"I'll bet you're the first Protestant Pope."

"Something like that."

"As I recall you were hardly the religious type. What happened?"

"It's a long story."

"Some people do some pretty dumb things. . . ."

On the defensive, I answered rather sharply, "You think it's dumb to be a minister?"

"No dumber than having a Ph.D. in biology. We're all treading water."

Sam hadn't changed a bit. He was the top student in math class. I remembered how irritating he could be by always having a quick answer for everything, and usually the right one too—the class cynic.

Then there was Fred, the football hero, looking as rugged and macho as ever, though he seemed a bit more paunchy than the rest of us. He lived in Florida now and still talked about the old game—how he scored a touchdown with six guys on his back.

John appeared. I had forgotten him entirely. With a big cigar in his mouth, he looked as grouchy as he always did, sitting alone, saying nothing. I remembered how he always seemed a little suspicious of people and careful about his friendships. He never smiled once all evening, displaying a total absence of humor.

Then there was Susan, the best date in the class. There she was, as vivacious as ever, table hopping, giggling, laughing boisterously, and demonstrating her femininity with a meek and shy husband in tow.

Faces, memories, reawakened feelings flashed by all evening, but when it was over and we were driving back to New Jersey, Joey and I talked about how predictable it all seemed. I recalled reading that at five years old our personality is set; at twelve our attitudes are fixed; and when we graduate from high school, our destiny is solidified regardless of vocation.

Most of us were already programmed before the mild and lovely June day on which we marched to our seats as my future wife played "Pomp and Circumstance." Some were pessimists even then. Now they spoke of our dying away; we would be fewer the next time we met. After a few drinks, they spoke of the harshness and emptiness of life with tears in their eyes, and I couldn't help wondering how they had survived this long in such darkness. Others back in our carefree days liked to be in charge. Loud, bossy, needing power over others to prove their worth to themselves, now they could be heard loudly reminding their spouses, "Not too much to drink dear; remember your ulcer."

Some labeled themselves not O.K. back in 1943 and for thirty years proved it to everyone as well as to themselves. In and out of jobs and marriages, and with few friends, they pushed you away with self-pity and an embarrassing remorse they hoped would gain sympathy and attention. Still others, the rich in countenance and confidence, the well-put-together, seemed to have it worked out. Positive about their own abilities, firm in their goals, clear about where they wanted to be (always near or at the head of the class), they were now the successful ones, talking of condos in Florida and trips to Hawaii.

I wonder what values influenced the outcome, shaped our personalities, and limited our visions and dreams: money, education, personal attractiveness, family, power? What semiconscious vows had we made to ourselves that we would never take back? Success at any price? Popularity at anyone's expense? How many of us at some high-school prom discovered how to manipulate the opposite sex for satisfaction and gain? Who envied the only student with a car and resolved to never do without as long as he or she lived? Who, angered by unpopularity, worked out happiness in terms of bank accounts, bonds, and bonuses?

And what of God? Could he gather up our frustrations, plans, obligations, and pledges to ourselves and use them to bring us to himself? What would he have to do to win us? How could he dampen our hopes, stop our plans, check our desires, increase our troubles, or multiply our blessings until we saw the enviable worth of having the loving God within? And how many of us did not have the ability to entertain the unthinkable choice of God because our perceptions of self remained too comfortable, too familiar, too secure?

For me the reunion was a revelation. I couldn't begin to adequately praise God for the immensity of my blessings, because I saw myself in everyone. All the crumbs of selfishness, envy, pride, greed, arrogance, and sloth I had within me. They are still there. But for some mysterious reason they were intercepted, hauled before the throne of grace, and miraculously did not determine the outcome of my life.

High school ended during World War II. We knew what awaited us. Some of my classmates who were already overseas in the military got their diplomas *in absentia*. At seventeen I could not be drafted, so my father decided that since colleges were receiving freshmen in June on their war-time schedules, I should go immediately on to higher learning.

College was a ball. During the summer of 1943, as I joyously discovered, there were ten women on campus for every male student. At the University of Connecticut my life was suddenly filled with a newly discovered happiness. I fell in love at least six times that summer, spent more time at sororities than I did studying, and to my regret, later joined a fraternity. I say regret because I found the fraternity system to be one of the most narrow-minded, heartbreaking, snobbish institutions I ever encountered. Meetings were usually spent picking over the lives of freshman candidates and sifting through the qualities that might make them good for the frat—intelligence, good looks, personality, complexion, religion (no Jews allowed), and money. It shocked my sense of justice and honesty. I saw young and hopeful men, who had been convinced of how necessary a fraternity would be to enjoy a lively social life, reduced to tears because they were not chosen. Later, when I briefly returned to the University of Connecticut after the war, I couldn't bear the warped judgment of the greeks, and to the surprise of many old friends, I chose to live in a dormitory.

In February of 1944, because of my active social life, I flunked out. I quickly enlisted in the Army Air Corps as a candidate for flight training. I arrived at the induction center at Fort Devens, Massachusetts, on a bone-chilling wet day in March. I had no overshoes, and after parading in the snow for two days in civilian clothes, I caught a terrible cold. My first two weeks in the Army were miserable, and I quickly learned to dislike military life.

Yet even there I found moorings. The Army gave me the self-confidence I lacked. The Army did not tell us that after arriving at basic training in North Carolina, fifty percent of us would be washed out and sent to gunnery school or the infantry on the basis of several days' testing. Up to then I hadn't done very well on tests of any kind, so I was surprised when I discovered I had escaped the infantry and qualified for pilot and bombardier school. By that time the Air Force had more pilots than airplanes, so instead of going to flight school, we were sent to an air base in Arkansas to wait until they needed us. After that, every six months for two years, a list of washouts appeared on the company bulletin board, neatly typed and precisely placed, instructing those chosen to pack their duffel bags for Fort Bragg or worse. Just then, the Battle of the Bulge made infantry replacements a high-priority item. Still I was never chosen. I must have achieved an incredibly good score on my tests. Soon we were down to less than five percent of those who so eagerly marched with us in the snow at Fort Devens. I began to believe in myself for the first time.

But I learned something else I didn't know about myself. For a time we worked the flight line on B-17's in Columbus, Ohio. Shortly after we arrived, my friend Josh and I got jobs as barracks firemen. This meant we each worked twelve-hour shifts tending the barracks boiler room, keeping the hot-water supply adequate and the heat going. I was crushed. I enjoyed flying as a crew member and working on the planes. I had caught on quickly and worked hard. Now I tended a silly hot-water heater in complete boredom.

Josh, on the other hand, was delighted. He didn't

have to get up and go out into the cold in the morning. He could spend his twelve hours in his bunk reading, playing cards, listening to the radio. He could stroll over to the dayroom and shoot a little pool. No one bothered him—no non-com on his neck. He enjoyed every minute of it. As for me, I sought every possible way to be reassigned to the flight line. One day while I was griping about it to Josh, he said, "I don't understand you. This is the best job on the post, and you're complaining. Relax. Enjoy it. Take advantage of the chance to sack out everyday."

I became reflective. What made me different from Josh? Why had I failed to appreciate the opportunity for an easier life? Did I have a compulsion to be where the action was? Or feelings of guilt because I didn't really have much to do? Or a need for people since the barracks day or night was a lonely place? Or was I a masochist who couldn't be happy with anything but misery, cold, and hard work? I concluded I was under some kind of compulsion, a restlessness, a drive that has never subsided in me. I needed, and always would need, work to do. Ease, pure pleasure, comfort, special treatment, self-indulgence somehow violated my victorian heritage; and I knew that I would never be anything but active, driven toward some goal that I had yet to discover.

When the war ended, we were among the first to be discharged; we seemed to be surplus material from the beginning. After a year or two of drifting in and out of college, collecting unemployment, and making a general nuisance of myself at home, I married a high-school acquaintance, Martha Allen (nicknamed Joey by a father who had wanted a son). She was the magic that turned me around in my academic life. With a working wife and a part-time job as a draftsman, I enrolled at the University of Bridgeport on the GI Bill. I graduated summa cum laude with a degree in mechanical engineering.

I had my start in the working world, which I had all along believed would be my lot. Yet the way things are as you go are not the same as they are when you look back. At that time if I were to have counted my gifts, they would have been quite different from those I now see were already in my life. I knew something of the sweet touch of the mystical. From my parents I had been given a strong sense of the moral, a respect for authority, and a feeling for what generosity could do for the soul. I was acutely aware that I had a passionate lack of passion, that I needed something that had so far eluded me. Restlessness, the need for fulfillment, and a few unexpected reminders of my own self-worth kept me from shrinking inward and prepared the soil in my heart for the seed that one day would overwhelm me with its life and wonder and joy.

Even then I was moved by a strange God who, through events, let me gradually see him in his mercy and in his glory, which is the only way we can see him and survive.

When my heart was grieved
and my spirit embittered,
I was senseless and ignorant;
I was a brute beast before you.

—————PSALM 73:21, 22—————

3

Intensive Living

A jail near Eyrarbakki, Iceland, lets its prisoners out every day to work with local farmers. The men return on their own each night at curfew. Once a tardy inmate pounded on the gate to be let in. The jailer reluctantly peered at the man through the bars and scolded him: "Next time you're late, I won't open the door."

One wonders what went on in the mind of the prisoner threatened with deliverance. Did he bang on the jailhouse door because he genuinely feared he wouldn't survive outside the familiarity of his cell? How many of us would be shaken if we were banished from the prisons we live in. A man buys a house in need of repair, and he spends every leisure minute nailing, sanding, painting, papering, digging, landscaping. It seems the needs of the house are endless. The house becomes an insatiable monster that entraps him with its possibilities—a bay window overlooking that beautiful crab apple in the yard; a rec room in the cellar, complete with bar for parties he never has time for; a green, unblemished lawn without crab grass and with built-in sprinklers—the opportunities are endless. The house becomes a prison, a neat excuse to avoid relationships, a place to spend time otherwise wasted, a projection of personality, a showplace of ingenuity. It's a matter of a soul made of shingles, picture windows, porches, and motorized garage doors.

Would it have been better if the man had lost his house a year after he got it—as a result of some financial failure that prevented him from keeping up with the payments; or a brief illness causing him to suddenly see the workhouse he had made for himself; or a new job that takes him to a different city? Whatever means the jailer might use to keep him from his prison, it would be better for the man to be banished and kept from all that sawing, planing, and painting. But he tenaciously clings to his lockup. In fact, he would be crushed if he lost it. He reports for duty; every vacant hour he pounds on the gates with his hammer and saw, to be admitted once again.

Translate this person's house into any similar commitment. The office, the business, the job—they all bring little fulfillment, lots of money, ulcers, colitis, heartburn, hypertension, and too much weight. The walls of this prison are made of overdue deliveries, production holdups, lost man-hours, risked money, labor problems, costly mistakes—and the pressure builds. But he dares not escape; bills need to be met, children educated, the mortgage paid, retirement saved for. The alternatives are too frightening: finding another vocation, reevaluating purpose and goals, making peace with God—all too scary. So the walls go higher. As the entrapment becomes complete, all opportunities of escape become unthinkable.

I'm convinced God can be the liberator, though it took a long time before I realized it. That is what I now preach. Yet whenever I speak of giving one's life to Christ, I often see the pain on the faces of those who hear me. I know that pain; on the surface, God seems to be asking too much of us. If I really follow Christ, what will I have to give up and who will pay the mortgage? What will I do if the boss asks me to lie about the next delivery? Can I survive on my job if I'm honest? Will my company accept the difference Christ will make? "No, you ask too much!"

I understand that fear. I remember sitting in the kitchen of a man who told me that Christ was urging me to love him and accept him. It was an impossible idea. It would lead to too painful a change in my purpose, goals, and achievements. I knew I could never make a decision like that—it was irrational, and I was too practical and sound-minded. I finished my coffee, thanked my host, and went home unchanged. I was happy with the prison I had shaped; at least I thought I was.

We moved to New Jersey in 1953. I found employment at Wright Aeronautical in Woodridge. I worked on a production model of a jet engine for civilian aircraft. Before then airlines flew piston engines, mostly on DC6s and DC7s. The engine manufacturers, Wright, Pratt and Whitney, and General Electric, were in competition to produce, test, and obtain FAA approval for the first American commercial jet. I was assigned to the stress-analysis section of engine design and went to Columbia University part-time.

Since I had received my bachelor's degree from a small college that had initiated an engineering program only a short time before I arrived, I felt I needed to establish my scholastic reputation at a more recognized school. Columbia seemed to be the only nearby institution offering a master's degree in engineering at night. Two or three times a week I traveled into the city. The most vivid recollection I have of the three years it took me to complete my degree was the plea *Save the Rosenbergs*. Julius and Ethel Rosenberg had been sentenced to death for stealing the atom-bomb secrets, and students rallied, hawked petitions, and shouted "Save the Rosenbergs!" at you the minute you emerged from the subway on 116th Street. I remember it because the demonstrations seemed overdone and pretentious for a cause that on the surface seemed to be justifiably resolved. Until then it hadn't mattered to me whether the Rosenbergs were executed or not. Now, I suddenly had leaflets about capital punishment, human dignity, and the cold war pressed into my hand, and a faint impression began to grow in my mind that many important human issues were beyond my consciousness. I became vaguely aware that I had isolated myself from the contamination of human feelings and sympathies; I had limited all my energies and studies to very specific technical goals. In the process, I had carefully eluded nearly everything that might widen my perceptions or enrich my personality.

The Rosenberg case filled me with mixed emotions.

Part of me resented the students for their indifference to authority. I felt they violated some unwritten code of respectability. But I also lamented for this couple who took such incredible risks for what they believed just. True, many misguided people with twisted logic had been responsible for terrible tragedies, but Julius and Ethel seemed different. They had two young sons who would have to bear the stigma of their parents' deeds for the rest of their lives. Besides, the death sentence, so irreversible and irredeemable, had an aura of hypocrisy and guilt about it because of our own use of the bomb against civilians. Did the Rosenbergs pay for our national conscience as well? My human capacities were still quite infantile so I couldn't sort out the justice or injustice of the sentence, but the Rosenbergs touched a nerve within me that reminded me of my embarrassing indifference to the human cause.

It would take a conversion experience to increase my consciousness about the poor, the handicapped, and the disenfranchized people of our world. I knew I had a capacity for ignoring the hurts of even those closest to me. It would take an inner revolution to remove that kind of ego from control over my life. I remember a friend who had an amazing gift of empathy, and though I admired his compassion, I didn't have the least desire to imitate it. Somehow I had entrenched myself in the falsely superior position of self-involvement that walled out even the most pitiable people. As I began my work at Wright Aeronautical, my training in the school of relentless arrogance continued at the graduate level.

My chief mentor there was a mad genius in charge of engine design. In his violent rage he drove everyone and everything before him. Often he would storm out of his office, cursing and screaming, looking for some poor engineer to blame for an unforgivable error. His face was livid; it seemed as though the blood pressure building in his brain would at any minute propel his eyes out of his head like bullets if his emotions put any more stress on his vascular system. What kept him from having a stroke or heart attack was impossible to say. We joked that he went home each night to beat his wife and kick the dog off the porch as a fitting conclusion to a joyless day. Ever since, I have used *kick-the-dog-off-the-porch* as a metaphor for all those internal nagging sins that result in outward anger, bitterness, and hostility.

Yet what he lacked in personal attractiveness he made up for in engineering skill, which probably only a pure engineer without emotions can best appreciate. He had, for instance, an innate sense that enabled him to locate stress in an engine part. He would stand back from the draftsman's board and squint at a design, seeking some aesthetic quality that would tell him whether it was structurally well designed. He believed that ugly designs with discontinuous, interrupted lines of stress-flow would be troublesome, and he was usually right.

But although he was right, brilliant, and acute, he nearly destroyed those who worked for him. He was an authentic mechanic. How I survived the insanity of that environment I'll never know, but I did. When confronted with a difficult relationship, we often endure it by taking on some of the characteristics of the adversary. (It is no accident that a husband or a wife will parrot the spouses point-of-view at times, even though wrong, distorted, or exaggerated.) From this furious man I learned some lessons that would take me several years to unlearn. They became a part of my character, learned out of self-defense and also because they worked; they got things done, which was the name of the game. I completely embraced Leo Durocher's approach to success—"nice guys don't win ball games." You can't have many human qualities and expect to get ahead. You have to be tough. Anything was fair as long as the job got done. You could lie, cheat, use your friends, manipulate, smile, or curse at the appropriate moment. It was quite all right as long as you came out the hero in the end, met the deadline, or created a successful product. I recall talking to a politician who had defeated us in an effort to build low-income housing for senior citizens. I confronted him with the arguments he used at a public meeting that were simply false, untrue, and misleading. "Well," he said, "you have to expect it; when you're in a battle you use any argument to win." When he said that I knew exactly what he meant.

Yet deep down I loved the work. I discovered a tremendous satisfaction in resolving technical problems. Given meager data about a structural failure, my co-workers and I worked through calculations and testing to find the weakness. In the test lab we would set up analogous situations, scheming up ingenious methods of analysis. I liked designing parts, seeing them work, interpreting data, improving the system.

Later in the rocket-engine business, I would never cease to thrill at the sheer power that consumed me every time I witnessed a firing, no matter how small the engine. Our biggest engine, with a mere fifty thousand pounds of thrust, was tiny compared to today's moon rockets. Yet when you stood fifty yards from the test stand, the low-throated roar not only hit your eardrums and penetrated your brain as sound, it also touched you. The sound waves vibrated against your body, your chest, your gut, and they gave you the feeling of being present in the very midst of power. This violent, turbulent force ignited something exhilarating within me as it pressed itself against my body.

Is there something within us that responds favorably to isolating violence? One time, many years later, I sought refuge from a youth dance where the volume of music in the closed reverberating room did the same thing, and I wondered if the people who danced in that deafening atmosphere, with strobe lights in semidarkness, weren't experiencing a similar sensation. Much later, when I began to appreciate prayer and contemplation, I found that even a loud automobile passing in the street could be quite disturbing. Our lives, from the moment of birth, are filled with a cacophony that shatters and keeps us from a peace we really never have or even know exists. Yet we seem to enjoy and even seek the thunder.

I worked at Wright for about two years. By then the handwriting on the wall told me that there was no future there. Pratt and Whitney's engine clearly won over ours. The sophisticated madness of our chief engineer, coupled with a system hamstrung by paper work, autonomous executives, and unyielding unions, had crippled us. Endless failures from a highly refined design couldn't be corrected fast enough or efficiently enough. I left Wright for Reaction Motors, a liquid-rocket-engine company in Denville, New Jersey, in 1955. It turned out to be the right thing to do. I moved up quickly in a growing company.

Early in our marriage, Joey and I lost our first child. Born prematurely at six and a half months, she lived only a few hours. Her death nearly marked the death of our marriage, a union in which we already suffered because of different goals, drives, unbearable interference from parents, and a sad lack of mutual maturity that caused us endless childish hurts, arguments, and despair. I recall vividly how close I came to leaving my wife forever after the nurse showed us our dead girl. I walked the ten miles home from the hospital, debating with myself about my future. For some incredible reason we went on. Looking back on that time, I'm sure we went on not because of any quality we brought to our relationship; we simply didn't have the courage for divorce so we stayed together. Though I don't believe marriages are made in heaven, it may have been the one right thing we did by the grace of God in those miserable early years of matrimony.

Three other children were born to us, all girls. Joey had several miscarriages between the three relatively normal births, and I would get angry and impatient with so much unexplained hardship and sickness. I had a certain self-pitying selfishness that became almost unmanageable at times.

I buried myself in work. We bought a house in Oakland, New Jersey, and we gradually added on to it. I did all the inside work, the plumbing, wiring, and finishing. I spent my weekdays working on engine designs and my weekends working on the house and yard, which helped me avoid both my relationships and my own questions about just what my purpose in life was.

At Reaction Motors I made a friend. We would ride to and from work together. I always regarded him a far better engineer than I, although, as circumstances would have it, he eventually ended up working for me. Sometimes, though rarely, I would deepen our discussion, especially when things got rough at work. I would ask, "What's it all about—the pressure, the headaches, the heartache? What am I doing this for?" But we didn't dwell on it too long. I guess we were afraid of the answers.

My friend would always say, "I don't ask myself those things. I just keep working and stay out of trouble if I can."

I had dreams but few visions. I suppose we all hope that our ambition will bring us what we need. But the trouble is that we are generally confused and misled about what we need. I seldom thought about such lofty notions as life's purpose. Instead, I had typical goals. I used to think, "Ah, when we get two cars, then we will have a little more freedom and happiness." We got two cars, and all the little inconveniences and petty irritations continued. "Well, just wait until we enlarge the house and have a nice fireplace to warm us in the winter and a beautiful patio to catch the cool breezes in the summer; then we'll be happy." I got the patio, fireplace, extra room, attached garage—in fact on a rainy evening I could drive into the garage and walk to the kitchen without even getting wet, which I considered high living indeed—and I was still impossible to live with. Then I thought, "Soon I'll be making more money. When I get my promotion, when I get the raise, that's when we'll really start to live." I got the promotion and the raise. But nothing changed. Augustine's famous observation "O God, our hearts find no peace until they rest in you"[2] was certainly accurate in my life. But at that time I had never heard of Augustine or the Peace of God.

I now consider my frustrating lack of satisfaction a great gift. Discontent prodded me to keep looking for something more satisfying. My restlessness reminded me of my incompleteness. My poor relationships made me increasingly uneasy about my own humanity. I seemed able to achieve anything I set my mind to, but I was totally unable to quench the thirst that dried up my soul. I didn't understand it then. In fact, it was a shock to discover that all my achievements had such little power to contribute to my happiness or well-being. I had succeeded as an engineer, but I continued to fail as a person; happiness eluded all my successes. There were opportunities for me to grow and discover something of the richer life, but I resented any intrusions on my privacy and my intense pursuit of fame and fortune.

In a very weak moment, I went to a picnic with a bunch of Christians my wife had befriended. I quickly became aware that they challenged my worldly superiority and self-righteousness with another sort of arrogance not much different from mine except theirs was shrouded in piety. I recall arguing with them about evolution. It was silly wrangling since none of us knew anything about the subject. Still I dogmatized my misconceptions, and so did they.

The most difficult moment came as we sat around a long table; twenty people satisfied with good, wholesome food. The self-appointed leader thought up a game to play: Each person at the table would tell what the most important thing was in his or her life. Of course, everyone gave the answers expected of them—Jesus Christ, church, Christian friends, the Bible, Prayer. My turn came. Obviously, I couldn't say any of those things. While I hesitated, every eye turned to me. Without much thought, I said that my job must be the most important thing in my life, because it gave me food on the table, a house to live in, and clothes on my back. Besides, I told them, I had recently received a promotion, so it had given me success as well. I mean, what else could be more important?

The group stared at me in awkward silence. I knew I had not said the right thing, and I inwardly cursed the idiot who thought up the game. I resolved to avoid Christians from that moment on. But also, because of that embarrassment, I resolved to avoid making people feel small, inferior, and foolish. Christians often make people feel that way by eagerly trying to project all the outward characteristics they believe a Christian should have. But they keep more people from the door of the Kingdom than they can imagine. At the time, that picnic reinforced all my misguided convictions about churchgoers. Yet I know now that those sincere, overzealous people also presented me with an opportunity to confront my behavior in relationships; at the time, however, I refused to contemplate it.

It was easy for me to see the inconsistencies and hypocrisy of believers—after all, I had been trained to spot weaknesses. But I didn't see that same subtle malignancy in the rest of the world. I had been completely duped by the conspiracy. I call it a conspiracy because I believe there exists a continual erosion of high principles in our world. I'm not talking about a personified conspiracy, like the Devil or the Antichrist, but a daily erosion of honesty, unselfishness, trust, reliability, friendship, and truthfulness. It exists because we convince ourselves these virtues would corrode and threaten our success.

For instance, one company I worked for prepared a presentation for the Navy in Washington. It included a progress report, and our progress hadn't been too impressive. But we had been summoned, so we had to go. We rehearsed in the chief engineer's office, reviewing the rules of the game:

—Avoid negative and harmful data whenever possible. Never, never volunteer information damaging to our success or reputation.

—Shade the truth if it would be to our advantage and we can get away with it.

—Tell them anything that will reassure them we have the situation well in hand.

—Blame other vendors whenever it seems advantageous to do so, and be prepared to back it up with engine test data. (You can prove anything with data—the same way you can prove anything with the Bible.)

—Always conclude with your personal, honest, and unmitigated opinion that all is well.

No one said these things aloud, of course; they emerged as an unwritten code. The point was that we couldn't be honest and survive.

But these lessons are everywhere for us to learn:

"It doesn't pay to be honest."

"If you don't take care of number one, who will?"

"You owe it to yourself to have the very best."

"Get away with everything you can, because you may never get another chance."

It's all part of the conspiracy to make us less generous, more suspicious, less willing to risk failure, less willing to help others, and more protective of what we have. At the time, I didn't understand that this conspiracy was a lie. The real truth appeared later when I

discovered that it is only when you take the risks of
opening yourself up, sharing, loving, giving, and reach-
ing out that you ever really grow as a person. A closed,
protective selfishness never leads to maturity. Instead it
promotes envy, fear, distrust, pride, jealousy, and hatred.
Jesus put it this way: "Whoever finds his life will lose it,
and whoever loses his life for my sake will find it."

What Jesus said was no pulpit cliché. It is true. It is
true of health: He who fanatically safeguards his body
becomes a hypochondriac; the mind completely focused
on itself becomes mentally ill. It is true of business: The
customer who is taken advantage of will never return,
but the customer treated fairly and generously will tell
his friends. It is true of friendships: A person enjoys no
friends until he becomes a friend. It is true of love: Love
given only to oneself becomes narcissistic and sick; love
given away grows rich and beautiful.

But I didn't care about maturity or relationships. I
cared instead about success, personal achievement, and
self-esteem. I was completely sucked in, convinced. My
life continued to be, at best, a quiet desperation. But the
events that lurked in my immediate future would bring
about a most blessed change.

But God, who is rich in mercy,
... even when we were dead ...,
made us alive ... with Christ.

—————EPHESIANS 2:4, 5 (RSV)—————

4

Grace

God grows flowers in a manure pile. He puts gulls in a garbage dump. He causes a seed to blossom in a crack in the asphalt. Geniuses—gifted people, great artists and musicians, child prodigies—impressive and awesome as they are, are not nearly as inspiring as righteousness emerging from corruption, hope from despair, insight from ignorance, life from deadness, benevolence from selfishness, and joy from grief. We expect the theory of relativity from an Einstein. We don't expect a Solzhenitsyn or Corrie Ten Boom from a death camp, a St. Francis from an aristocratic family, or a Charles Colson from a Watergate.

People met an unexpected Jesus when he went back to his home town. The incident suggests that this local kid hadn't always acted religious when they had known him as a boy. The butcher, the baker, and the candlestick maker, shocked by his words in the Temple, said, "Wow, wasn't that Mary's son? The same kid who let Sam Levy's mule into Ruth Cohen's garden? Who, instead of working and supporting his poor widowed mother, was always dreaming and wandering off somewhere?"

God surprises us. He puts to shame our religious preconceptions with the people who bear his banners and become citizens in his Kingdom. That is why the Bible is so believable. It portrays Kingdom people with all the crumbs of corruption we see everywhere. Jacob, the original used-car salesman, becomes Israel. Moses, in a temper tantrum, kills a man; then he brings a whole nation out of slavery and into the promise of God. Saul, intense and bold, determined destroyer of the tender beginnings of the Christian faith, becomes Paul, still intense and bold, but the determined instrument of God. Peter, weak without courage, becomes a rock. Thank God he doesn't rely on the intelligent, gifted, successful, respectable, beautiful people; his Kingdom, made up of beggars and cripples, allows for us all. Well, by the grace of God, he included me, though unrighteous, among the righteous.

One quiet night, shortly after the birth of our second daughter, Joey became convinced of God's presence in her life. She became a Christian. She also became unbearable to live with. She played hymns on the old piano in the cellar, went to church (of all things), insisted on grace before meals, bought a Bible, started going out every night to Christian meetings, prayed at the most awkward moments, watched Billy Graham on television, and worst of all, tried in vain to ravage my well-ordered life with the most oppressive religious clichés she could muster. I ran for cover. I worked as many hours as possible and read Bertrand Russell in self-defense.

During that time, God used a young man named Phil Bandstra as a means of his grace in our lives. Phil, a laundry and dry-cleaning deliverer, stopped regularly at our home. I can imagine what the neighbors thought when they saw his truck parked in the driveway for hours. But Phil was genuine. His strong Calvinist background didn't inhibit his warmth and humanity. He had an incredible ability to turn any subject to religion without being offensive or self-righteous. He wasn't afraid to let you see him; his peeves and impatience showed. He readily admitted to kicking the dog off the porch. But God was in Phil. Without applying pressure, and without a sickeningly superior self-assurance, he talked about God (not to me as yet, but to Joey). He answered questions, spoke lovingly about the Scriptures, described his church, laughed affectionately about his family and himself. He enjoyed his children, cherished his wife, and loved the Lord. I seriously doubt if either Joey or I would have become a part of God's Kingdom without him.

When I beat a hasty retreat from all this holiness, Phil cautioned Joey to lay off. Prayer would do it. I think they had every Christian in church praying for me.

That was the summer of 1957 when Billy Graham came to Madison Square Garden. As I recall, his original schedule kept getting extended so that instead of spending only a few weeks, he actually remained for most of the summer. For several weeks Joey expressed an interest in going to the city to hear him. She finally did go on a bus with a church group. Our oldest daughter, who went with her, later told me about that wild ride into Manhattan; her mother had paraded up and down the aisle praising God, singing hymns, and making a general nuisance of herself. I was at home, babysitting, and I was thankful for having an excuse not to go.

As the summer wore on, Joey talked incessantly about *both* of us going. She, Phil, and others gently pressed me. Time was running out—in August, only one more week of Billy Graham's Crusade remained. Prayers were said; hopes expressed; strategies planned; schemes discussed. I didn't stand a chance against all that intrigue. Three days before the crusade closed, I consented to go.

Joey wisely arranged for us to ride with the Bandstras. She knew a Bible-thumping, hair-raising ride on a bus full of hymn-singing Christians would have sent me to the nearest bar the minute we arrived at the Garden. She must have had a thousand people volunteer to take care of the kids, and she had asked every available Christian to pray for the outcome.

The Garden was packed as usual. We sat up high in the mezzanine, for which I was grateful—I had learned long before I became a Christian never to sit in the front. There were the usual hymns. Cliff Barrows led the choir. George Beverly Shea sang his songs. Then Billy began his sermon on Zacchaeus. Safely removed from the action, I folded my arms in patient superiority. I don't remember the details of his talk, but I suppose he spoke of how Zacchaeus turned to Christ and was saved from his sins. All I remember now is that as he talked I felt very peculiar; I felt drawn to something outside of myself. It was a sensation I had never experienced before. I was gradually overcome by a sense of goodness, a marvelous beauty that I had never previously known. Everyone in that place was suddenly my friend and my benefactor. I was overcome by feelings of worthiness, joy, and compulsion.

The only words I remember Billy spoke were those Christ said to Zacchaeus who was perched in a tree to see Jesus: "Zacchaeus, make haste and come down."[3] As Billy talked he waved his hands at the balcony. He clearly meant me. Stunned and afraid, I leaned over to my wife and asked her if she would go with me. At the same time, other people began to file forward in response to Billy's invitation to give themselves to the Lord. It seemed like a dream. Somehow I was out of control, no longer propelled by my own will. I stumbled down the stairs and ramps and made my way to the floor where people were gathering. What happened immediately after that remains vague and mixed with intense and conflicting feelings. I know I went behind the auditorium seats somewhere, mingled with the crowd of "new-borns," met with a Christian counselor, and discovered Phil and Marge waiting nearby. They were full of praises and thanksgiving.

Back out on the hot summer New York street, it was quite a different story. Sanity began to seep back into my brain. I thought, "My God, what have I done? How would I explain this back at the office? What will my friends say?" As we walked back to the car, Phil and Marge stayed behind, not saying very much, almost sensing the fragile condition of my salvation. I sternly and unfairly ordered Joey not to mention to a soul what had happened. How hard it must have been for her not to tell people. It reminds me of when Jesus told the cripple who walked for the first time in his life not to tell anyone about his healing. As the man departed, leaping and praising God, Jesus must have smiled to himself, realizing the impossibility of his command. Joey must have felt cheated by my request for silence as her feelings urged her to leap down 32nd Street, ready to praise God to any poor soul who happened by.

To this day I find it difficult to understand and explain what happened that night. My friend with whom I regularly rode to work saw no difference in me the next morning; I wasn't about to tell him what mad escapade occupied me the night before. At work I acted the same; intense, harsh, anything's-okay-as-long-as-the-job-gets-done attitude. (Actually, I didn't know any other way to act.) No one could have seen the difference in me, because I stepped back into the same routines—indeed, I never slipped out of them. I had heard of dramatic rebirths, of people whose lives were never the same again. But my life seemed no different. Those people experienced a continuous ecstasy and joy. I had the same short temper and impatience I always had. Those people talked of Christ to everyone and gave up their sins. I wanted to talk to no one about it and still had all my sins.

As I look back I realize how careful we have to be about our expectations of the process, methods, and schemes God uses to save his people. The amazing thing is that God is more willing to take a risk with us than we are with him. He gathers us up into his Kingdom, with all our depravity and sin. He recognizes we will continue to embarrass him, frustrate his purpose, resist him, battle for the wrong causes, and desecrate the temple where he struggles to be within our own hearts. He understands all these things. Still he takes us in as if we were lonely, bedraggled derelicts on the front stoop at five minutes to midnight, and he fully knows we are not to be trusted. But if we think God will not accept our ungrateful, miserly little souls just as they are, we are mistaken. There might, in fact, be so much corruption that it would take another lifetime to resolve; yet he accepts us anyway. I recall how hard it was to quit smoking. I threw the cigarettes out the car window. I stamped them into the ground. I took pills to make them taste bad. I cut down to five a day. Nothing worked. I was at the mercy of tobacco. Sometimes our sins are like that. If that is the case, and if we are willing, God doesn't wait for us to kick the habit; he takes us addictions and all.

Something quite irreversible happened that hot summer night in Manhattan. God wasn't finished with me yet. Even though, on the surface, this hardly seemed to be grace, his gifts were to come to me relentlessly in some of the most trouble-filled days I had ever experienced.

5

Trouble

Charles Fenyvesi, an editor, gardener, and carpenter, writes, "Nature abhors the straight line." He points out that nature consistently conspires to bend and undo the persistence of men to produce straight lines. A door sags; a road is forced around a mountain; an airplane is pushed around a thunderhead; rain and ice cause a road to buckle. The straight line, he says, is a "permanent and unalterable value; a first solution, direct thinking." Curves include "hills, branches and rainbows"; they are "hospitable to excess and fantasy, pleasing to the eye, a love poem."[4]

I think Charles Fenyvesi has hit on something. In fact, I would take it further—*God* abhors a straight line. He is forever shattering our straight-line thinking, our dogma, and our best-laid plans. We crave cherished absolutes. We would like it very much if life were mechanical and predictable, if meaning could be found in the practical, if we could rely on things and commodities and people. Instead, he shatters and shakes our assessments, footings, resolutions, and systems. He keeps reminding us that our bank accounts and houses and cars are not enough; each dismally fails to humanize us. He desperately wants to convince us that what we seek to buy and save up and protect is dust. There are no straight lines to things that last or give us hope or reinforce our dreams.

Well, if God loves curves and alternate routes and poetry and hills and valleys (Isaiah 55:12), he had selected for himself a straight-line personality in me. I used to think that if a thing wasn't practical, it wasn't worth any time; no poems for me. If you had something to say, then say it so there would be no question about what you meant. No one had time to search or discuss or contemplate the fire of genius. Zoology, sociology, economics, psychology were the best academic electives; never literature, art, history, language. No time for idle chatter. If you talked it had to mean something. It had to be profound and practical and enlightening. The best solutions always proved the most direct, the way of least resistance, the least costly, the most productive. When something had to be done, you did it—or you had someone else do it. If he didn't do it, you reprimanded him or fired him. There were no deviations, no excuses.

Some religions deal with straight-line personalities, religions that would have us believe in simple solutions to the human tragedy. They allow no room for doubt or fear of the unknown; they describe God in understandable and definitive terms; they would dogmatize love and friendship and beauty and truth; they adore certainty and reliability. I could not accept that sort of religious assurance in spite of my impatience with the subtleties of life. I had been trained to doubt. No bit of data could be accepted at face value. No system could be designed without backup, fail-safe devices that prepared for the inevitable failure. No test firing could be presumed successful without carefully checking all the results. Questioning saved us mistakes, and mistakes were costly.

So God had a problem on his hands. I was a person who liked direct, clear, precise thinking but who could not accept a God who was so precise and definitive that he was impervious to question and doubt. It seemed to me that if God really did exist, he must be in categories and visions and dreams that I had not yet examined or discovered.

It was a wonderful gift that God understood my religious apprehensions and didn't leave me on a New York sidewalk outside the evangelist's tent. He continued to prod and urge and push me in ways that were not easy or manageable. He began his instructions in faith with my father's death.

In the fall, my father, who would be the most resistant and hurt if I ever renounced straight-line methods, became sick; it appeared he needed a gall-bladder operation. At seventy-two years of age, he entered the hospital for the first and last time in his life for an operation. He handled the surgery beautifully, but an inoperable malignancy was discovered. No one told him of the finding. After an initial recovery that amazed us all, he became ill for the last time in October. He died in his own bed the day after Christmas, 1957.

It was a period of suffering for all of us. Avoiding the words *malignancy, cancer,* and *inoperable,* we lived with half truths, superficial conversations, promises that couldn't be kept, and discussions of a future that would not be. To this day I believe we made a mistake. Avoiding truth belittles people; it cheats them of opportunities to prepare themselves; it is terribly presumptuous and self-serving; it fills the last irretrievable days with lies and fears and lost opportunities to cling and hold on to one another. I didn't tell him what had happened to me on a hot night in August, because I didn't have the nerve, and because I feared he would disapprove of my actions. I was afraid of hurting him on his deathbed.

My mother asked him if she could invite her Episcopal priest. He refused. Circumstances, whatever they may have been—overbearing dogmatic preachers, overzealous Christians, undeserved suffering, the enlightenment of Charles Darwin, the free-enterprise system, his own physical handicap—combined to shape him so that he died outside of Christ—at least, outside any public acceptance of Christ. What went on in the man's mind during those final weeks and hours, none of us knew. He never let us see his emotions, moral conflicts, hurts, confusions, joys, or celebrations of his soul. I never saw him naked until the day he died. And then I saw him shriveled and alone and unknown.

For many reasons he had a tremendous influence on my life, both good and bad—not unlike any parent. But as we stood around his bed, watching him gasp for breath, I privately vowed not to die that way. So alone.

Few knew him. No friends. No one holding hands. No prayers or tears or hymns or hopes or joys that peace at last has come. I knew then that ergs and oscilloscopes and slide rules and British thermal units would not be enough for me. I knew that in his moment of death, a part of me was near death too. The vital organ of my humanity lingered on the edge of the grave.

Even in those last weeks of my father's life, I could not speak of things that both of us wished we could have shared together but did not know how. I realized how much of my person had been choked off. My laughter and tears were inhibited by an unwritten restriction on emotion. The sharing of my inner feelings with others was restrained by a fear of criticism. Self-doubt disabled any crusade that might have ensued from my most heartfelt convictions. The impulse to show affection with a pat on the behind, a hug in the park, a kiss at the bus stop was quieted by my fear of losing my machismo and dignity. As we stood around his bed, I saw clearly for the first time how boxed-in all of us were, unable to come to terms with our emotions, feelings, and fire. Christ would yet lead me to love and share and come to terms with myself. While I grieved his passing, my father's death proved a liberating experience.

Pressure began to build at Reaction Motors. I had been assigned to the Corvus missile. It was designed to deliver enough explosive to an enemy radar installation to destroy it. It would be launched from a Navy attack airplane, the A4D. Clearly, we were in the business of war, making military hardware. My conscience was stimulated, and I thought briefly about a possible conflict of faith and work. But as noble as such thoughts might have been, they were short-lived; my preoccupation with our technical situation became serious and all-consuming. Our engine failures began to threaten the whole system. Pump and component weaknesses in the engine plagued us to such an extent that we couldn't accumulate enough test experience to know whether we would ever meet our specifications in efficiency, thrust, vibration, weight, and so on. All the other vendors seemed to be ahead of us. We had exceeded our budget and completion date. The Navy was getting nervous. Temco in Dallas (the prime contractor) was nearing prostration. And our own superiors were breathing down our necks.

My own work focused on a single engine component, the combustion chamber. We began to make real progress in that area; pressurized running (without the pump) showed a remarkable durability for that part of the system at least. As for the rest of the engine, it seemed to be experiencing one problem after another. And then one day, the chief engineer summoned me to his office to announce that from that moment on, all of the Corvus troubles were mine. I was now the chief on that engine system. I was an official project engineer with private office and personal secretary. I had arrived. I could now assume all the responsibilities, failures, technical problems, financial overruns, and pressures of the job. For the next nine months I ate, slept, dreamed, stewed, suffered, and fought that engine through to a successful flight test off the California Coast.

But it wasn't easy. We tested through three shifts, working fourteen-to-sixteen-hour days. Even the few hours I had left to sleep were often interrupted with phone calls from test-stand engineers with questions about what to do when things didn't work right. I fought with everyone. The shop foreman, production manager, metallurgists, design engineers, vendors, quality-control people, chemists (fuel analysts). I had a reputation for ruthless success. I made enemies, but I got the job done.

And I traveled. Flying regularly between New York, Dallas, and Los Angeles almost made an alcoholic out of me—I had a fear of flying. I don't know why. I flew in the military and never gave it a second thought. I loved it then, even though people got killed in all sorts of accidents. But my fear of civilian aircraft became so severe that I began arriving at the airport an hour ahead of schedule. That gave me enough time to get sloshed at the bar so I would have the courage to get on the airplane. Once on board I would drink all the way to my destination. I would also plan to arrive late enough in the day so I wouldn't have anything to do but go to bed and sleep off my drunken state. Then I could make myself presentable at the job the next morning.

Some of my fear may have been justified since I had more than one close call on commercial aircraft. One instance convinced me of the unpredictable nature of flying. A Lockheed Electra Turbo Prop, newly introduced and widely touted for its ability to get to efficient operating altitudes in a hurry, nearly did us in. We left Newark Airport for Dallas, Texas, late one sunny afternoon in a brand new airplane. The flight was quite uneventful until we encountered a thunderstorm outside of Dallas. We flew through the most turbulent weather I had ever experienced—sudden, sharp changes in direction; unseen forces gripping us and pulling at the plane. Even with our seat belts fastened, we had to hold on to the back of our seats to keep from being pitched forward or sideways in the turbulence. Without a doubt, it was the most frightening twenty minutes I had ever experienced on an airplane. It improved my prayer life immeasurably.

On the ground at Love Field in Dallas, my gratitude was ecstatic. It was late evening when I made my way to the motel and went to bed. The next day the evening newspaper reported that the very same airplane, on its way from Dallas to Houston, fell apart over Buffalo, Texas. Everyone on board was killed. It would be two years and several accidents later before researchers determined that the engine mount bent just enough during the thunderstorm to induce a sympathetic vibration in the wing, causing it to break up. That day I calculated that, including wind resistance, it would take several minutes for someone to fall 30,000 feet from an airplane after its initial disintegration. Plenty of time to think! I shuddered as I wondered what would have gone through my mind on the way down. Perhaps just one long scream as I plunged into eternity. I had not yet progressed far enough in my Christian faith to consider if it had been by God's grace that I made it to Love Field. But I was supremely thankful I had not died that way.

I wasn't much of a father or husband in those days. I hardly saw my family, and most of the time I was short-tempered, irritable, and inconsiderate. My mind was on other things. My wife left me alone, happy to see as little of me as possible when I was in a bad mood. I did, however, begin going to church.

It had been nearly twenty years since I had been there, not counting the few times I had gone to early Mass with a few drinking buddies after an all-night New Year's Eve party. Many times I saw my wife go off on

Sunday morning in tears because she went alone to celebrate the resurrection or birth of the Lord.

But now I had joined the Reformed Church in America simply because it was available, the only church in town. I suppose if it had been Methodist I would be a Methodist now. I had never heard of the Reformed Church, and it didn't really matter to me what traditions it followed. Our pastor, a man in his seventies, had lingered past his effectiveness, especially in a growing community like ours. But I liked him. He had a touch of enthusiasm and drama and vigor about him, as if he had long ago caught a vision of the Kingdom and it still lingered within him, though tarnished and shop-worn with the years.

The church leadership thought of me as ripe for the picking, so I became involved in Christian work. I found myself sitting impatiently through all sorts of committee meetings. Since I was an engineer, they tapped me as finance chairman and fund-raiser for a new building we were about to build. I was quickly made a deacon, serving a three-year term on Consistory (the local board of trustees). Strange, isn't it, that the church, the very place where you would expect to go to deepen your faith and contact with God, spoke instead of bricks and mortar and bonds and fund-raising events. It became the place where I was lulled into believing that I was pleasing the Lord when all along I wasn't doing anything different than I did at my job; except it was all done a lot less efficiently.

I found myself adrift in pettiness, dollars, and mortgages. Sometimes I found it to be unbearable non-sense. I recall one Consistory meeting where the debate raged for two hours over how a door should be planed down and rehung in the Sunday-school building. Many meetings satisfied the ego of some poor man (women weren't allowed on the Consistory yet) who, not having any power elsewhere in his life, inflicted himself on us by slowing things down to be recognized—a sort of ego-building exercise through the power of negative thinking.

I often became exasperated with what I found in the church. Not knowing what I needed to grow as a Christian, I floundered. I hoped something would happen to enlarge my spiritual life. Once someone from work called me while I was at one of those insufferable meetings and remarked to me later, "That's the first time I ever had to call a church to get an answer to my problems." He expressed a truth he didn't recognize. It is understandable that not many people call the church about their problems and needs. The irony is that the church and Christian people did not bring me any closer to God at that point—but secular events did.

After several successful flight tests, our engine went into formal testing for Navy approval, and we prepared for production. Gradually we began to relax a bit. We still had a few problems meeting low-temperature and vibration requirements and a few shipping troubles, but at last we could see the light at the end of the tunnel. I had succeeded, at great personal sacrifice, in turning what looked like sheer disaster into imminent triumph. But quite unexpectedly events changed course, and I would never be the same again.

One bright, cheery morning, I went to my desk to discover a telegram from the Navy in Washington, D.C. It read, "Please be informed that the Corvus program has been canceled. No further testing, shipments, or work will continue. . . ." After I had gone through booze, sweat, and tears, some bureaucrat decided we didn't need the system any more. The project ended. It was over. I was stunned.

Religion is commitment. The Christian religion is commitment to Jesus Christ. But on the basis of commitment many things could be classified as religious—the Communist party, a weed-filled lawn, sexual pleasure, a bank account, the stock market, vegetarian diets. It suddenly occurred to me—my religion had been the worship of pumps, propellant tanks, valves, combustion chambers, and occiograph readings.

When I had time to think about it, that telegram made me realize how foolish, misdirected, and misplaced my allegiances had become. It reminded me of all the sacrifices I had made and of how far I seemed willing to go. What shocked me the most—the truth that loomed most vividly before me—was my willingness to jeopardize my health, family, marriage, and sanity for tubing, bearings, ceramics, and fire. It was as if that telegram said, "Now do you see how irrational and trifling life can be? What you were ready to give up the most cherished values for isn't on anyone's list of needs or dreams." Later I walked casually through the shop where I had spent so many hours threatening, begging, complaining, griping those engine parts to completion. I now found my beloved hardware being sawed into scrap. Overcome with the absurdity of life, I vowed to reconsider my presuppositions, principles, and purpose.

God was present in the death of my father, at Madison Square Garden, in telegrams from the bureaucracy—could he speak any more clearly to me? I saw more then than at any other time in my life how God uses events to redirect us according to his will.

Clearly others were as affected as I was by the cancellation. What did they see? They saw a very annoying end to another government job. They saw the frivolity of the military. They saw new opportunities for other work. They saw a possibility of layoff and began to tighten their economic belts. They did not see God.

When the Egyptian armies drowned while pursuing the Israelites, some people thought it was a result of some natural disaster like a tidal wave. Wars won against the Philistines were seen by some as the result of military power and clever generals. A convicted criminal was executed on Golgotha—some thought it just and said good riddance. The same events were seen by different observers, but the conclusions were antithetical.

What induces some of us to see God in drownings, victories, executions, and telegrams? We see God because he touches something within us that is never the same again. Somehow he gives us a new organ, a separate set of eyes that like the newborn's blink and frown and wonder at all the blurred images, bright lights, and strange shapes. But somehow we see and begin to interpret events and happenings in a new way. We see because in a hundred ways he has nudged us and prodded us and pried at us to see telegrams differently from everyone else. With that telegram in my hand, it occurred to me how important that blind, stumbling, groping trip from the mezzanine had been.

Looking back, I could say those couple of years were fraught with trouble. I had experienced the death of a loved one, alcohol as a threat to health and happiness, alienation from family, the near destruction of a marriage, cancellation of a big contract, and possibly a lay-off and loss of work. But for the first time, those enigmatic words of Paul "We also rejoice in our sufferings"[5] began to find a responsive echo in my life.

Troubles *can* be a blessing if they lead to faith. If they drive us to God in search of meaning, purpose, strength, then they are a blessing. Troubles can be a blessing if they force us to ponder life. Many times people have told me from their hospital bed that they've weighed their lives and seen how they have allowed vanity to steal away their health with expensive toys and intense living. Troubles can be a blessing if they bring us to our senses about ourselves. The younger son, filled with youthful fantasies and ready to be somebody, went to a far country to become a nobody—in a pigsty. It was as if the pods the swine ate mirrored his greed, false superiority, and insensitivity toward his inheritance, traditions, and father's house. There, among corn husks and slops, he vowed to go home. Troubles can be a blessing if they lead us to new conclusions about our values. Nothing is more illustrative of this than death. Sitting at the bedside of terminally ill people in their final hours, we realize the obvious fact that all of us are ultimately reduced to a condition in which no medicine, no knowledge, no wealth, no status, no strings will help us. We are reduced to one precious value alone—God. So if troubles cause us to recognize the value of the inner life over the value of outer appearances, then those troubles are a blessing.

Again, by the grace of God, I began to have another look at my life. Even though I was assigned to an exciting new project and a heroic new goal—Surveyor, and the moon.

"You will decide on a matter,
and it will be established for you,
and light will shine on your ways."

————JOB 22:28 (RSV)————

6

Pivot Point

We had never seen anyone actually living in a rain forest, but we had the impression it would be a nice place to visit. While traveling in our Volkswagen camper through the Olympian peninsula in Washington, we veered slightly off course to see what high rainfall can do to protected vegetation. We are some of the few who would prefer other vistas of nature.

As we moved from the sunlit parking lot into the forest, darkness eagerly threw itself around us. As we followed the prescribed trail, the moss-laden dampness struck our senses. The smell of penetrating moisture reminded us of moldy shoes, rusted tools, and mildewed tents. Trees, heavy with growth, bent down like green stalactites, almost touching the marsh as if to weld the vast growth into one impenetrable world of vegetation. The sounds of elusive slithering and plopping seemed to be a part of the green silence, stimulating our imaginations to conceive what sort of creatures lived in the bogs and quagmires. As we penetrated the forest more deeply, an unsettling sense of separation from the familiar and comforting overtook us. We were strangers in that forest. We felt unwanted. We didn't belong.

Isn't it strange to think of nature as unnatural simply because civilization has adapted us to dryness, to light, and to cool air in summer and warmth in winter? We had long since left the wilderness. We had isolated ourselves within the cool detachment of air conditioning. We were familiar with places where neither summer nor winter changed our habits. We lived with windows shut, doors closed, storm windows in place to keep out the elements, protecting us from the discomforting reminders of the natural world. As we hurried back to our camper to seek a more pleasant environment, we were aware that the rain forest had made it quite plain that we had become completely civilized.

Driving away from the dampness, I also realized that, while it seemed unreal to us, everything in that forest was fulfilling the law of nature in the real world. If my sensitivities had been offended by nature's moisture-laden thicket, with its frogs and moss, I wondered if I had been deprogrammed about other chunks of reality as well. I thought of the British colonel stopping at midafternoon in the hot, sweaty jungle. Pitching his tent and preparing tea for himself, as if denying where he was, he would contradict the surroundings with his civility. And had we done the same with God? Had we denied reality because we thought we belonged to a system that didn't allow him space in our scheme of things? Had we become so civilized, important, and knowing that God had become as unreal as old wives' tales, leprechauns, and rain forests? We now drank our tea brewed on an electric stove, in a kitchen warmed by a super efficient gas boiler, in surroundings fitted with every conceivable gadget to make living easy. How could God be real to us, let alone a necessary part of our plans?

Aldous Huxley wrote somewhere, "The advance of natural science, logic and psychology has brought us to a stage at which God is no longer a useful hypothesis . . . a faint trace of God still broods over the world, like the smile of a cosmic Cheshire cat. But the growth of psychological knowledge will rub even that from the universe." I had believed that, until a rain forest forced me to consider how a pseudocivility, personally fashioned, had seriously impaired my vision. I began to discover that oscilloscopes, voltameters, and pressure gauges did not describe the most important parts of reality.

For some this might not be a revelation, but for me it was a tremendous insight. I recognized that spiritual qualities like love, wonder, creativity, and laughter would never be given, weighed, or measured by any exact means. Up to this time I had been convinced by those scientific television commercials that my undershirt was clearly whiter with Brand X than it was with Brand Y. Now I began to wonder about the value of such whiteness as well as the values of those people who are convinced of the need for such radiant washday miracles.

My Christian growth could best be described as a liberating experience. I no longer embraced a stubborn selectivity of the rational alone. I became aware of a new consciousness. I began to smell roses for the first time. I experienced deliverance from selfish opinions and cherished convictions. I gradually felt the light around me emerge and reveal human tenderness, poetic truth, new adventures, and visions. Reality took on a new vastness that I had not known existed.

For instance, I began to see qualities in people other than the practical side of their character. Previously the plumber, the cop, the professor, the housewife all performed a service that I could rely on, learn from, and use as I had need. Now I gradually began to see warmth, attractiveness, and genuineness in other people. I began to see their struggles and to better understand the reasons why they were who they were. I had never seen that before, partly because I had viewed life mechanically and people as functions, and partly because personal doubts had consistently caused me to look for something in other people to criticize, condemn, mock, laugh at. Now I became aware of an ingredient in some people that seemed special and new and immensely satisfying. I discovered that in some intangible way a unity and commonness connected me with others.

One incident in particular challenged my stereotypes. It was only one of many difficulties Joey had with her pregnancies; the memory of several miscarriages still linger in our minds. One night she suddenly hemorrhaged and caught a three-month-old fetus in her hand. She called to me and woke me out of a sound sleep. I nearly passed out with the shock. Men, in those days, were not well-trained about such things. The Lamaze Method was not yet widely practiced and the last person the obstetrician wanted in the way during the pain, blood, and birth was the cause of it all—the husband. Completely unprepared, with fear and trembling, I called the doctor and took her to the emergency ward.

So when she became pregnant with our third child, we were apprehensive that she might have trouble again. Sure enough, at three months, severe pain erupted in the night. In the morning we went to the doctor. The obstetrician examined her and concluded she had a tubular pregnancy. She needed immediate surgery to remove the fetus. Any delay meant an increased risk of death from internal hemorrhage. We hesitated. He suggested another opinion. The second specialist confirmed the diagnosis of the first. Within an hour Joey was admitted to the hospital for immediate surgery. Overcome with anxiety, I kissed her and then watched the nurses wheel her into the operating room.

In the car our two children began to cry. We were all afraid. I drove home. I sat at our kitchen table and remembered no one had had any breakfast. It was now almost noon. The doorbell rang. A neighbor asked if anything was wrong. Confused by panic, lack of sleep, hunger, and dread, I clumsily told him the story. He came in, sat with me at the table, and prayed. I had never actually heard anyone pray for me before. Deeply moved, I felt warm and good about his caring. I was partly reassured Joey would be all right. He took care of the kids while I raced back to the hospital. When I arrived, I was informed that both specialists had made a mistake. In surgery, they had discovered a normal pregnancy; the child was correctly placed in the womb. In another six months she became our third girl, born normal and healthy. She was a joy. After that near-tragic day, I began to see dimly a quality of love in people that I had never given them or myself credit for.

I began to change in other ways as well. I discovered the value of literature. I had believed that if it couldn't earn you a buck, it wasn't worth bothering with. So Chaucer, Shakespeare, and Coleridge were wasted on me. I never understood the value of the classics until I realized many authors asked questions and raised issues I needed to ask and consider in faith. In reading, I recognized that their questions were the same ones I had been asking although I had never verbalized them. I read Steinbeck, Camus, Sartre, Miller, Baldwin, Dostoevsky, Tolstoy, Hemingway, and many others. They talked about guilt, war, sex, prejudice, violence—all the human tragedies and predicaments—in ways that stunned my consciousness. I realized this newly discovered Christian faith I had embraced couldn't hide from such vivid illustrations of mortal despair. Modern authors had outdone Calvin in stating the case for total depravity; now it seemed to me that Christ would have to supply the alternative. I realized that if Christianity could say something significant about the dilemma described by the great authors, it could be a bulwark for any man or woman's troubled life. I explored the arts, music, and poetry. I discovered a whole world I had relegated to dust on my shelves.

I vowed never to close my mind to anything again, and I began to get excited about a religion that didn't fear or ignore the most troubling issues. In fact, what use was a faith that remained unexposed to and protected from the storms and assaults that would crush it? Bigotry, wars, atom bombs, alcohol, drugs, vandals, small-mindedness, dogma—whatever would threaten faith needed to be experienced and met. I believed that with such passion that my entire world view began to take a form that startled me with its hunger for testing, answers, and adventure.

Of course, I began to read the Bible. I gradually learned to love it for its honesty, humanity, divinity, and for the characters it described. I was especially awed by the offensive stories it preserved. I thought some promotional expert might have easily edited them from its pages long ago to make it more pleasing and salable. But by some mischievous miracle, they had been preserved—for what discomforting reasons, I didn't altogether understand. Perhaps they were there to test our willingness to struggle with their audacity. Perhaps they troubled us by reminding us of the distinction between God and men. Perhaps they had shock value, producing awe, wonder, and contemplation. There is the story of Uzzah who was struck dead as he put out his hand to steady the ark of God that was being drawn by stumbling oxen.[6] And Agag,[7] a willing prisoner of war, glad to be alive, cooperating with his captors, but suddenly and viciously hacked to pieces by Samuel, God's interpreter. And Ananias and his wife Sapphira[8] who suddenly died because they withheld for themselves what belonged to God.

All these stories spoke of enigma and tragedy interpreted, rightly or wrongly, by faith. But they spoke also of the genuine human and divine struggle. A word from the Lord emerging from the riddle of human events seemed much more believable than the idea that in some unexplained manner the Bible appeared out of heaven. And the idea of God incarnating himself in the fallible human heart fascinated me. God, though holy, is conniving to become a part of the unholy, compelling us to repent, sending after us the "strong, sharp-toothed sheepdogs of the Great Shepherd to thwart any desire, foil any plan, frustrate any hope until we come to see nothing will ease our pain, nothing will make life worth living, but the presence of the living God within."[9]

I began to feel that an important quality God must have was his being at odds with our culture, our cherished ambitions, and our most noble achievements. The pages of the Bible revealed just such a God, a God who interrupted the lives of men and women who often resisted him and sometimes staggered under the burden of his choosing because he seemed so opposed to their most cherished assumptions. The God of the Bible didn't always smile like some maître d' receiving a generous tip from the faithful. This God blessed the rejected, named the last first, defied all our systems that would grind up the underprivileged, disabled, tender, innocent, disenfranchized people. This God called the unrighteous to righteousness, in spite of failures, enabling his unlikely candidates to rise to a level of integrity far beyond their highest hopes. This God remained in the darkness for our sakes. This God gave the kind of optimism that didn't dismiss the darkness. This God didn't stifle and oppress us with dogma, routine, and ritual, but he came often in banquet and picnic, eating and drinking and laughing. This God had a sense of humor; even those most familiar with its pages often fail to read the Bible with the awareness that it sometimes speaks with celestial wit. I gradually fell more and more in love with the Scriptures and with the God it described.

I didn't lose my job. I had done my work well. We

saved a lost cause. Corvus flew. The unpredictability of generals and admirals wasn't our doing, so I moved on to another project—Surveyor. Moon exploration had just started. NASA needed to land delicate instruments softly on the lunar surface. Only impact landings had ever been attempted. Our part in the project included the development of three small variable-thrust rocket engines to fine-tune the final landing descent.

Again I got caught up in my work and travel. But I became extremely cautious about the importance of what I was doing. My value system had changed, and I knew that something far more important than rockets and moon probes and space travel gnawed at my soul. I went to worship services without fail; even when I traveled I found a church to go to. Often I personalized the sermon, Scripture, and hymns, sometimes reading a verse that touched me several times through. I came away more and more convinced of a destiny not yet within my vision.

Once I went to a meeting at which four or five widows told about how they had followed their slain husbands' paths to a village in the Amazon, to the very people that had taken the lives of their men. I remember being awed by their courage—a courage I knew I didn't have. They witnessed to being led there by Christ, and who could have denied it? Such audacity, faith, and foolhardiness spoke of grace. Well, I needed some of that boldness because I never considered myself a courageous man. I remembered once how some kids had hung a rope from a huge maple tree. They would climb up to the first big limb that stuck out from the trunk; standing on it, they held onto the rope and swung out into space with laughter and thrills. I managed to get to the starting point and hold on to the rope, but I never pushed myself off. I stood there with everyone urging me to go until finally, in shame, I climbed down to make room for the next eager swinger. I knew if I ever found the courage to push off in life, it would have to come from outside myself—a passion, a devotion, a cause to follow—and I knew Surveyor wasn't it.

I honestly don't know when the thought first entered my head; perhaps I merely drifted toward it. It certainly wasn't logical. My salary in 1960 was $16,000. We had completed our patio, fireplace, two extra bedrooms, attached garage, and driveway. We had two cars. I had an established reputation as a successful engineer—an achiever. I knew almost instinctively what to do to solve a technical problem, and I loved it. There was no reason to give up. No personal emotional crises consumed me. No passion, other than a continuing sort of restless dissatisfaction, troubled my soul. But somehow, some-where, I began to think of going into the ministry. I thought of seminary.

It seems strange now, but I never seriously weighed the sacrifice. I never felt threatened by or fearful about the consequences of the decision to change vocations, even though up to that time I had never made an impractical resolve in my life. Now as I look back, it seems as if I am watching a motion picture of someone else going through the drama. I wonder, "How could that be me being that daring and foolish?" But as I lived it, there seemed nothing special about it at all. The thought that haunted me was the fear that I might be working out some subconscious plan of escape from business pres-sures. I knew what I had been through on Corvus: the booze, the fears, the endless hours of work, the alienation from wife and children and friends, the sheer frenzy for success. I didn't want that to happen to me again. Not until I could satisfy myself that I wasn't looking for greener pastures did I really move ahead with the change. Perhaps what convinced me most was that Surveyor went well. So far I had handled it without letting it become my possessor.

In the summer of 1960 my feelings for change became more intense. One hot Sunday night, Joey and I sat quietly on our new patio with the lights out. The kids had gone to bed. A gentle summer night's breeze was especially welcome after a humid afternoon spent working to screen in the porch. We had a magnificent view of the Ramapo River Valley below us. In the evening haze, house lights twinkled on, giving us the joy of distant life. Behind each light we could imagine a family laughing, crying, searching together to make it all work—not unlike our own. I broke the silence with the sudden question, "What would you say if we went to seminary this fall?"

I surprised myself with my own words, but I was more surprised with Joey's unhesitating response. She must have seen it coming because she said simply, "I would like that very much." I couldn't believe such a loaded question could receive such an unadorned answer.

It was decided then, almost like a decision to have a cheese omelet for supper or to paint the bedroom rose instead of pink. And I suddenly realized the real saint in all this was Joey.

Saintliness is more than purity, piety, and reverence; it is the quality of sacrifice more than anything else. You don't have to be a saint to give up ice cream if you happen to dislike the stuff or even if you're indifferent to it. The tough thing is to give up ice cream when you are the kind of person who goes to bed at night dreaming of banana splits. All my life I had been indifferent to money, fine furnishings, fashionable clothes, and picture windows, and in recent months I had sensed a deepening of that indifference because my achievements and possessions failed to satisfy my restlessness. Somehow Tiffany lamps, Eldorados, and breakfast at the Tower Suite, while I might enjoy them for the moment, had no lasting quality and gave me no satisfaction. Nice to have them, but I wouldn't miss them if I didn't.

But Joey was different. Her mother raised her to believe the best was none too good for her daughter. She had been carefully schooled to appreciate fine linens, silverware, furnishings, and clothes from Saks. Yet she consciously gave them up. No fanfare about it, no regrets, no agonizing, no compromises; I knew what it cost her, and I was humbled by her willingness to begin the journey. Possibly she didn't understand all her motives for agreeing anymore than I did, but she was the one who sacrificed her dreams and heart's desire. She took the risks, not I. She caught sight much more quickly than I did that we had been touched by something special, that that something was worth every risk and sacrifice. She saw the vision of all the hopes and joys that lay *ahead* of us. Our marriage, our life, our situation had been far less than ideal; now maybe there was a chance for something better. Now, instead of drudgery, heartache, noncommunication, petty arguments, daily frustrations, there could emerge a quality of life that had eluded us. She grasped, better than I did, all that lay ahead of us, and for that hope, she gave up far more important dreams than I had.

We rented a cottage at the Jersey Shore, hoping to get

our thoughts straightened out. We had a beautiful two weeks together. We enjoyed the beach, the surf, the smell of the sea. We ate fresh-caught flounder, swam, talked, and planned. I made a quick trip to New Brunswick where, surrounded by the State University Rutgers, the Reformed Church in America Seminary has resided for over two hundred years. New Brunswick essentially consisted of Hertzog Hall, a huge archaic building housing the offices, dormitories, kitchen, and lunch room. The structure seemed to be a foreboding anachronism. It loomed and glared at you from the top of a modest hill. I often wondered what Rutgers students thought as they walked by on their way to class. The hall must have reinforced their notions about the church— dusty, quiet, dignified, austere, and pretentious. As I watched them, I felt sure I could see a slight quickening of step in the seminary block.

I recall entering the president's office. It was large and sparsely furnished, with a dusty, threadbare oriental rug on the floor. On the walls several reverend clergy stared forsakenly from portraits at all who dared to enter. My first lesson about the church sank in immediately. This was a far cry from the plush and extravagant corporate offices I was used to; and I knew the difference was money, not sacred asceticism.

The dean of students met me. He seemed preoccupied, gripping a sheaf of papers in his hand as he came in to greet me. He was cheerful enough, but he didn't encourage me. I don't blame him; I was too much of an unknown, an outsider, for him to be anything but skeptical.

"So you want to become a minister, do you? Tell me

why." He smiled again. This time with a touch of cynicism.

I didn't want to tell him the whole story. I sensed he wouldn't understand Billy Graham and tent meetings. So I said something like, "I feel a growing sense of lostness in people, including myself, for something meaningful. People, I find, are detached, and they know it but don't quite know what to do about it. I want to help find a purpose . . . a direction. . . ."

"You think you're going to do that here?" he interrupted my groping, hesitating answer.

"I hope I'm going to learn how here."

"Well, we've received your records from Columbia and the University of Bridgeport, and your grades are certainly adequate, but you have no philosophy, language, or history. You would be lost here. I think you had best reconsider."

Ignoring his remark, I pressed him further and said, "Assuming I'm determined to go ahead, the earliest I could start would be the second term in December. Is there any way that could be arranged? I have to sell my house. And then there's the matter of finding a place to live down here. I would need to start on that right away. Anything to suggest?"

Misreading my question, he answered, "Well I could suggest some readings in philosophy and history. Then you'd have to do something about Greek. . . ."

For some reason what he said didn't discourage me. I drove fifty miles back to our cottage and thought about his warnings. Could I make it in disciplines I had always meticulously avoided? Greek? How could I ever pass Greek? And what if I quit my job and didn't make it? Could I go back to Reaction Motors again? Surely not to the same job; I certainly couldn't expect that. All these thoughts ran through my mind as I looked forward to doing a little more vacationing and thinking by the sea.

I suppose when you make a decision as monumental as that, you ought to remain as rational, unemotional, and calculating as you possibly can. Certainly, if our children came to us with some wild scheme, to climb Mount Everest or go to Alaska to live in a log cabin, we would give them pretty cautious advice. "Have you thought to pack your things? Do you have your rubbers, earmuffs, and money belt? What if you run into unfriendly natives? Suppose you go so far you can't get back? Who will show you the way through the thickets and forests?" Thoroughly rational people do not take risks unless it's all thought out.

Yet how often a couple comes along who seem too young for marriage and announce their matrimonial intentions with no income, no service to render, and no visible means of support. To all our logical reasons for restraint, they counter, "But we love each other!" And all reason collapses in the presence of the beloved. The immense risk seems small to them as they cling to one another in the sheer joy of new-found love. Listening too intently to reason defies the passion. Prudence rarely takes into account the fire. Good judgment puts everything in its place; it catalogs and makes lists of the arguments and denies the joy. Why must we have logical, practical reasons for everything we do? Psychiatry lures us into thinking we have motives for every action, that our inner world runs by cause and effect like some Newtonian formula. So we incessantly seek motives and explanations. And fearing we have none that will satisfy the mechanic, the logician, the analyst, we hesitate, search, reconsider, falter. Absurd, isn't it? When the very nature of life, God even, loves extravagance and the preposterous. Possibly the *only* reasons are His.

By some incredible power, we made the choice. As I look back now, I wonder how a sober engineer, trained to calculate, plan, define, and count the costs, could have done such a thing. It wasn't rational. It wasn't courage. It wasn't dedication. It certainly wasn't through the encouragement of others. But we did it. We did something so absurd that it had to be God.

When you think of it, it isn't in God's nature to be reasonable. No wonder most people try to keep him out of their lives. Is it reasonable for a person to deny personal comfort? Is it reasonable for a person to want the world to be just when he or she is personally guilty before the bar? Is it reasonable for a person to want to *see* the imperfections? Isn't ignorance better than insight?

It seemed to me faith always contains a fragment of the irrational. The space scientist attracted to the complexity of the adventure says with faith and conviction, "We *can* put a man on the moon!" He says it fully knowing there is no proof that he can. He says it knowing that he may find nothing of value when he gets there. He says it even though it's possible he may not live to see it happen. But he says it. Why? Any faith has an element of audacity. So does faith in God. To put it in George Macdonald's words, faith has the "haunting scent of unseen roses."[10] Without that, we would never commit.

I wrote a carefully worded letter of resignation to my boss at Reaction Motors.

After very serious consideration I find it necessary to inform you that I will be leaving Reaction Motors on December 1. I wish to express my appreciation to all concerned for a very satisfactory and enjoyable relationship with the company over the years. My decision is based on personal considerations that lead me into a completely new field of endeavor and is not founded on any discontent with my present position within the company.

Again, I wish to emphasize that my relations with everyone at Reaction Motors have been excellent, and it will be difficult to take leave of the many friends I have made here. I trust that the date of termination is satisfactory to you, and I will appreciate any attention you may give to this matter.

The deed was done. I had made the move. I put our house up for sale. I would begin seminary on December 1, 1961.

People who heard of my decision reacted with different intensity and opinions. My mother was appalled. She called Joey and asked, "Can't you talk some sense into him?"

A peer at work confided, "I sure see your reasons for doing something besides what we're doing, but your solution is ridiculous."

Our family doctor couldn't believe it. "You're going to seminary? I can't imagine how they would let you in!" He knew something of my drinking and my callousness.

A chemist in the lab at RMD said, "I envy you."

An inspector in quality control responded, "I didn't know you were a Christian—you always seemed so severe, without warmth, unfriendly."

There was a big office party at which I was sent off

with booze, speeches, and gifts. But to most people my decision seemed emotional, unconvincing, and foolhardy.

I read Will Durant's history and a summary of philosophy from Socrates to Kierkegaard. Bob Marsh, the new pastor at our church, tutored me in Greek and was the only person who encouraged us on our way.

My family joined me at seminary in March of 1962. At first we couldn't find a place to live. Finally I discovered a little house for rent in Edison, New Jersey. I inspected, repaired, and cleaned it before we moved in. I replaced a window missing in one of the bedrooms, removed a kitchen cabinet door that hung by one hinge, and scrubbed out the sinks and toilets. The house, built on a slab of concrete, had radiant heat that later proved completely inadequate. It wasn't ideal, but it was a place where we could live together as a family.

Moving day arrived. We scrubbed, vacuumed, and polished, making our house ready for the new owners. As the moving van pulled out of our driveway, we pressed one anothers' hands, and with tears in our eyes, we locked the front door for the last time. A neighborhood couple accompanied us to Edison, helping with last minute arrangements, caring for the kids, and bringing some miscellaneous articles in their car. As we approached Edison on the Parkway, a freak March storm suddenly raged up the New Jersey coast. It started to snow. When the van arrived, six inches had already fallen. The movers, anxious to get home, simply moved everything into the house without asking where it belonged. Boxes and furniture were everywhere. The storm raged outside. The furnace ran and ran inside but failed to warm us. The new window I had put in the bedroom fell out; snow came in on the bed. We gathered with our friends in the kitchen, where we managed to get the heat up to an acceptable level by using the gas stove, and we ate greasy hamburgers and soggy french fries purchased at a nearby diner.

It was late. Our friends, too, feared the increasing snow. We hugged one another. We cried. We parted. We felt alone and terribly forsaken and insecure. We asked God to guide us. We went to bed that night with our clothes on, huddled together in the same room, wondering if our critics were right and we had done something completely insane.

If the trumpet does not sound a clear
call, who will get ready for battle?

──────1 CORINTHIANS 14:8──────

7

Blowing the Trumpet

In Bar Harbor, Maine, Joey and I hiked down to the ocean and perched on the huge boulders that make the Maine coast famous for its ruggedness. It was a magnificent day—the sun warmed us; the gulls circled above; and the quiet sea swirled among the rocks, searching for some lonely crevice to fill with its foam. Distant sailboats enjoyed the wind; still-more-distant ocean-going ships plodded across the horizon. We lived through a few moments of joy and peace—one of those rare times when we felt close to the earth and to him who created it. Nearby a cormorant worked at catching fish with an all-too-familiar intensity. I had never seen a bird like that before. Large, with a wingspread of thirty-five to forty inches and not very attractive, it swam about searching for food. Suddenly it would nose down and disappear completely below the surface. I timed its dives up to a minute and a half. Bursting from the depths, mostly without success, it would swim around to regain its breath before diving again. Maybe once in every ten dives it came up with a catch, quickly swallowing the fish. We watched it for thirty minutes, admiring its persistence, endurance, and concentration. I was glad for those moments. It enabled me to see in nature something of myself. Intense, preoccupied, obsessed, compulsive, this big bird that seemed to achieve little for all its efforts reminded me of myself.

Finally, the show over, it flapped its wings to take off for more fruitful fish-laden currents. But as hard as it tried, it couldn't get airborne. The bird would skim along the surface, flapping and spraying salt water as it went, only to settle back on the sea like Howard Hughes's Spruce Goose. Frustrated with itself, it would shake wildly like a dog coming out of a stream and try again. Several times it tried unsuccessfully to rid itself of the sea, until finally, with one tremendous effort of huge wings beating the air for support, it lumbered away, skimming majestically along the surface, gaining altitude slowly, and at last managing to disappear around a bend in the coastline. I admired that bird as it left us and silently prayed for better fishing.

In a way that cormorant described the next few years of my life. Lots of energy, persistence, determination, but not very many fish. It even depicted a period when I tried to fly on to something else but never succeeded, flapping, and complaining that I had become waterlogged, deadened, and wasted.

Seminary went well. I managed to struggle through Greek and Hebrew and enjoyed theology, church history, Bible, and practical studies. We were nearly the oldest couple on campus, and soon our apartment became a center of activity. The coffee pot forever brewing; fellow students incessantly at our door—we loved it. At the end of our second year we were given a summer assignment in Park Ridge, New Jersey. The minister at Pascack Reformed Church had moved to another church, and the congregation needed a temporary student while they looked for a new man (women were not ordained then). We packed our three kids and everything we would need into a 1957 Volkswagen and drove to middle-class suburbia where we were met at the parsonage by one of the parishioners. The church had furnished the house with the essentials, stocked the refrigerator, and welcomed us gladly into their fellowship.

We enjoyed that summer. I discovered I actually felt good about preaching and writing sermons. That was a minor miracle. Back in my engineering days, I didn't consider myself a public speaker at all. On rare occasions when I had to make a presentation to other engineers or marketing people, I usually became so self-conscious that I couldn't get my own name straight.

That summer in Park Ridge I lost most of my fear of public speaking, though I don't think one ever completely loses it. But I learned never to apologize for a sermon. I preach with this attitude: "This is what I've got to say this week folks; it's the best I can offer you; it's honest and it's mine, so here goes with no excuses."

And I liked the church. We hit it off immediately. By the end of the summer a delegation from the congregation told me they would be willing to wait until I graduated if I would accept a call to their church as the next pastor. Of course, I was flattered, but as a student I couldn't accept a call until January. They were more convinced than I that my future would be shaped in Park Ridge, so convinced, in fact, that at one minute after midnight on New Year's Eve they called to formally offer me the pastorate at Pascack Reformed Church. I accepted, having done some pretty thorough soul searching and exploring of other possibilities. I became convinced that I could work through this all-white, middle-class suburban church. At least it would be a good place to start since I felt I understood their concerns, attitudes, and aspirations. After all, I, too, had commuted five days a week to an office, traveled incessantly, and tried to find a proper balance between earning a living and being a husband and father. Here, I felt, God would have me work. My ordination took place in the Pascack Reformed Church in June, 1964.

At the time, the country was in the midst of moral and spiritual crises. Kennedy had been assassinated. Vietnam began to be more than a skirmish. The "greening of America" had begun. The hippies, the yippies, the beatniks, the long hairs, and the dungarees began to shock the sliver of America I had chosen to identify with. The church at large was in turmoil. It became almost schizophrenic. It attempted to identify with the revolutionaries because their causes and slogans seemed Christian. But at the same time, it desperately tried to remain in the good graces of those who paid the bills—the middle-income, successful, mostly white wage earner against whom the kids reacted.

In many ways I, too, felt a part of the protest. I agreed with what the young, the hippies, and the blacks said about our society. Our most promising leaders had been shot. Prejudice had deeply embedded itself in the minds of most people. Once again war seemed to be the easiest political solution in a country whose name many of us had never heard. Most of the power, wealth, and leadership had failed to provide solutions or alternatives for the poor and powerless. So my preaching concerned itself with the issues that seethed around us, issues that had to do with the quality of life and our religious faith. I couldn't read the New Testament without seeing the validity of radical action for peace. I sympathized with nonviolent demonstrations.

Yet my loyalties remained with those whom I epitomized—the middle-aged wage earner. After all, I knew about the midlife frustrations of the average male. Much of the animosity and anger between the generations at the time resulted from youthful perceptions of what success had done to the working man. Lucrative jobs didn't necessarily lead to a life filled with meaning, self-respect, or high principles. Many of us, as an outgrowth of the depression, put money, job, and success before personal growth, inner strength, personal peace, or human relationships. Many found themselves in eight-to-five jobs in tight little offices; sifting through such important documents as purchase orders; answering to aggressive authoritarian personalities in high places; worrying about tuition, mortgage payments, and the fees of automobile mechanics, dentists, and doctors.

The kids saw this. They criticized our compromises and widened the generation gap. One man told me he had thrown his son out of the house *permanently*. The last straw had come when, during a violent argument, the son asked his father why he allowed his life to be wasted on such unfulfilling work—work through which the father had clothed, fed, and educated his son. If work were an entrapment for him, the old man argued, it was because he had unappreciative kids to feed. With only the slightest hint of regret, he told me he hadn't seen or communicated with his son in a year.

Too often, however, I saw the pain on a man's face who had allowed his work to deprive him of his humanity. I could sympathize because I, too, nearly allowed the same thing to happen to me. I looked back into the pit from which my life had been redeemed. Like Scrooge seeing himself in his dreams guided by the ghost of the future, I saw a small-minded, unhappy, selfish man living out his days without the courage or knowledge for doing anything about the boredom, frustration, and emptiness each day seemed to bring him.

Once a woman told me that she didn't really know what her husband did since he retired except snooze and listen to the stock returns on the radio. No one needs to wonder why the final years of a man's life are not used to find God, especially when a man has leaped at every opportunity to enrich his bank account and avoided every opportunity to enrich his soul. He who does not know himself to be already dead—how difficult it is for him to find life. The years of personal achievement, driving success, and the stockpiling of goods have gradually worn away the last meager crumbs of the spirit where God might dwell. Such a man approaches death not knowing how to allow himself even one brief moment of glory. Denying a lifetime would be too much for him to contemplate or imagine.

Old men are not easily evangelized. They have long ago shaped, cemented, and carved their destinies.

Thomas Merton wrote bluntly about the choices we make, "Why should anyone be shattered by the thought of hell? It is not compulsory for anyone to go there. Those who do, do so by their own choice, and against the will of God, and they can only get into hell by defying and resisting all the work of Providence and grace. It is their own will that takes them there, not God's. In damning them He is only ratifying their own decision—a decision that He has left entirely to their own choice."[11] Many of our youth saw the hell their fathers lived in and resisted any idea of following in footsteps that led to that kind of oblivion.

But I could never completely side with those who criticized, marched, and condemned. To me these seemed to be days of arrogant righteousness, and my view of good and evil failed to see the clearly defined distinctions others so quickly outlined. I could never quite bring myself to the point where I could draw a line and say everyone on this side will go to hell and on that side will go to heaven. For me the sheep and the goats milled around together in the herd. Alexander Solzhenitsyn wrote in *The Gulag Archipelago*, "If only there were evil people somewhere insidiously committing evil deeds, and it were necessary only to separate them from the rest of us and destroy them. But the line dividing good and evil cuts through the heart of every human being. And who is willing to destroy a piece of his own heart?"[12] I felt part of the same mixture of sin and goodness, and I could see it everywhere. It is said that only those who see things in distinct black and white act, and that those of us who see the shadows and the hazy sun peering through everyone and all human events fail to take sides or act as the prophets "in the name of the

Lord." Yet often the choices seemed to be between shades of gray or the lesser of many evils. I had no illusions about righteousness. Who of us, after all, can understand the inconsistencies even within ourselves? Only God understands the evil he has allowed us to become so that we might be good through his grace.

If any goodness appeared in my life, it came after Christ became a part of it. Only by the grace of God am I righteous at all; and conversely, only by the grace of God am I kept from self-righteousness. I discovered over and over again that the Lord conspires to show me the bits and pieces of every man's sin within myself, especially when I begin to feel superior. If I condemn violence a little too supremely, something happens to cause me to explode with emotional violence. If I become smug over another man's indifference, someone with a problem interrupts me, and I find myself reacting inwardly with resentment for the intrusion. The minute I even slightly enjoy criticizing someone's self-importance, somehow, somewhere, my dignity and position is overlooked, and I feel hurt and ignored. I simply never get away with self-righteousness and quite rightly can never quite decide where the Kingdom starts or ends. The final judgment on us all will require divine wisdom indeed.

But more than anything, one early experience cured me of virtuous public demonstrations. In my senior year at seminary, one of our most militant classmates organized a march on the city of New Brunswick in the name of civil rights. We paraded through the rain into the downtown shopping area, singing "We Shall Overcome" and "He's Got the Whole World in His Hands." New Brunswick has plenty of blacks, but none were marching with us. We hadn't even consulted them. No one had appointed us to be Jeremiah, Amos, and Hosea. Clearly, we lacked the vulnerability, personal sacrifice, and sensitivity of the prophets. As far as I could figure out, all we managed to demonstrate was a childishly high opinion of ourselves and low opinion of everyone else. There had been no specific problem or incident to protest. We simply said, "Hey everybody, look at us; we're not prejudiced like you." At that time our seminary had one part-time black student, no Hispanics, and no Orientals. I imagined that those shoppers wondered what we thought we were accomplishing by parading around in the rain, and I knew that any real civil-rights advocate who knew the details would be picketing the seminary.

Though I tried to be cautious about involving myself in self-righteous demonstrations after the New Brunswick march, I was not altogether successful. I am sure, for instance, I went to Park Ridge with more than a little smug religious virtue. I imagined, like so many who graduated from seminary in those days, that I would be the one who blew the trumpet with such a distinct sound, with such enticing persuasion, and with such irrefutable logic that no one would misunderstand and resist assembling for the battle (1 Corinthians 14:8). Believing in those early days the Christian faith had something to say about the issues, I pressed those issues on the congregation for consideration and action. In spite of occasional displays of arrogance and virtue on my part, some responded in a positive way to the turmoil and testing of the times.

For example, we circulated a good-neighbor pledge, a promise to sell our houses (when we were ready to sell) without regard to race or religion. This circulated among the congregational families in 1968. I recall being cor-

nered in the local diner by one of our parishioners who
was retiring and selling his house. His wife sat next to
him, nodding her head in agreement. He said, "The only
thing I really worry about as we prepare to leave this area
is *who* will be living in my house. I got myself a good
realtor who knows how to attract those I want and
discourage those I don't want." He drove his point home
with his chin out and his finger poking at my chest.

But thirty-five people did sign the pledge. As I
looked at the names of those who had committed
themselves I knew how difficult it was for most of them.
They had grown up with the same prejudices I had. All
those years I had heard conversations that categorized
Jews as rich, untrustworthy, swindlers, and blacks as
lazy, with inferior intelligence and offensive diets. Prejudice doesn't disappear without conscious effort. Certain
things we learn we never really escape. In our mind we
may come to know something about right and wrong, but
in our gut we almost never get rid of the feelings we try to
consciously reject. For example, I grew up with the strict
notion that movies and the Sabbath should never occur
on the same day. Humphrey Bogart or Mickey Mouse
could not entertain on Sunday. To this day I have
feelings of discomfort when I go to a movie on the Lord's
Day. Now of course, I have learned those feelings are
unjustified and untrustworthy; it is likewise with much
of our prejudice.

Another blowing trumpet came at the height of the
fighting in Vietnam. I preached against the war, especially the invasion of Cambodia and the B-52 bombings of
Hanoi. From the pulpit I asked people to write the
president as a way of protesting our country's actions; a
small minority responded. The night the final peace

came (when U.S. involvement ended), eight of us gathered in the church, hugged one another, said prayers, sang a hymn, and rang the church bell.

In 1964 our church could have displayed the Good Housekeeping Award. Everything was in its place—no dust, dirt, cigarette butts, candy wrappers, or fingerprints anywhere. We had succeeded in keeping it that way because no one used the building from Sunday to Sunday except for a few church committees. We had a big facility: a church school with twelve rooms; a 5,000-square-foot church hall with stage, kitchen, coatroom, eight lavatories; a church sanctuary dating back to 1812; a choir room; four pianos; a parking lot for seventy cars; a vacant lot for the overflow; and seven acres of unused cemetery land. I calculated an average use factor of three hours per week per 15,300 square feet of building space. It had to be a sin to be that overindulgent and exclusive with church property.

So we opened our doors. I contacted Alcoholics Anonymous, and they started a group that met every Friday night. It grew rapidly, alcohol being a problem in our area. We managed to scrape enough money together to put an indoor basketball net in our church hall, certainly not an uncommon thing. But we agreed to let kids from anywhere in our town play without supervision—an incredible achievement if you know anything about church boards that endlessly concern themselves with liability and property damage. We took the risk, and in fifteen years we never experienced a single incident of abuse or injury. Although the endless ringing of the door bell to get the key to the hall touched my impatience at times, I more than received my reward when, years later, the grown players remembered our church as a haven they couldn't find anywhere else.

We opened a youth center with the intention of attracting troubled kids; *they* almost did destroy the building. About all we consistently drew were troubled cops who gave us statistics of high vandalism on the nights the center was open. We began to be approached by all sorts of groups for the use our buildings: bridge clubs, transcendental meditation, Vietnam veterans against the war, junior women's club, Boy Scout banquets, Girl Scout meetings, hospital auxiliary fund raisers, Eagle Scout ceremonies, marching bands, Yoga classes, and so on. We included all we could fit in, charging them what I am sure were less than our expenses. Once I was shocked to see the face of the Maharishi Mehesh Yogi staring at me from a local store window and inviting people to a transcendental-meditation meeting with the caption "Pascack Reformed Church." But we used the buildings. Later I began to see differences between our church building and others. We no longer shone with Dutch Cleanser. Things began to look threadbare, but our use factor was no longer painfully embarrassing.

While we accomplished much in those early years, my restlessness and intensity must have provoked many people. As we focused on one aspect of faith, others got neglected; we simply weren't doing much to help people with personal problems. In some ways we deepened them. These were the years of the generation gap when you never trusted anyone over thirty. Though I was well over thirty, I sided with the kids, sometimes for the egotistical reason that they responded more readily to my style of ministry. But by doing so, I probably wrongly aggravated the misunderstandings. I often made the mistake (like many others in those days) of believing the world could best be run by children who lacked depth, reliability, perception, and (most seriously) the experience of pain and compromise.

But I had other problems, too. I found many church people were faithful to church as a person might be faithful to a favorite television program or baseball team. They tuned in occasionally to find that nothing had changed, the same manager and the same team played the game without much excitement or enthusiasm. Some preferred it that way—there is some comfort and security in esteemed sameness. But most people had come to church, at least in the beginning, hungry for a sign of hope, a healing word, a brief glimpse of promise beyond an unpredictable and care-filled life. And these people we had failed. Preaching was ineffective. The causes we promoted didn't have much to do with what was hurting the average churchgoer. Even those things we did do to help people could be found elsewhere.

For instance, though I felt my professional training in counseling and caring had been adequate and worthwhile, I couldn't really see why a secular counseling center would be any different from ours. The overwhelming thought that I couldn't get rid of was that the church had forsaken its uniqueness for something else. All the religious trappings and symbols were powerless because many church leaders were powerless. Most people knew it even if they couldn't verbalize it, and they couldn't say it because they had been led to believe that what they were experiencing *was* religion, Christianity. I began to take all this very personally. I knew I was powerless, too, because I knew the congregation's emptiness and hunger was mine as well. So far I had neglected my own inner light, a light I was only beginning to see might also have an impact on the troubles life imposed on us. I began to think that maybe there was hope beyond professionalism, an assurance beyond counseling sessions, endless committee meetings, and sermons about our prejudices.

I couldn't help recalling the incident in the Gospels that put our best schemes and causes in a perspective we religious people sometimes accept begrudgingly.[13] After the woman of Bethany had poured out her love for Jesus in the form of an expensive ointment, our Lord proclaimed that her love would forever be a sign of authentic belief. Wherever in the world the gospel is preached, she would be a mark of its credibility, he said. The poor could not be served without this portent as well: a wildly audacious love for Christ.

This woman of Bethany reminded me of our failure to be enthusiastic about what we believed. Our skeptical observers all too often noticed the inconsistency between our sometimes outrageous claims for the Lord and our lack of boldness in faith and works. All too often they clearly saw the emptiness, boredom, and lack of passion in our prayers, our worship, and our commitments because we lacked this "beautiful thing" done to the Lord. But more than that, the secular professionals saw the naïveté and ineptitude of our politics and our programs. After all, they had more power than we to affect the causes we promoted because they had the money, the cunning, and the influence we lacked. I quietly pondered how we could demonstrate in a credible and believable way this one unique quality available to church people—the venerating, careless love this woman showered on Jesus. At the time I had no idea how to authenticate our words and actions with the holy sign of the incident at Bethany. But a man's illness gave me further incentive to find a way.

By chance I met a woman who asked me to drop in on her husband who resided in a nearby nursing home. He was forty years old and terminally ill with a brain tumor. He had had surgery, but the doctors could not remove all the malignant tissue. Now it seemed a matter of months before he would die. She informed me she would have nothing to do with religion, but she knew her husband had a deep desire to go to church and probably would have if it were not for her influence. Quietly and privately he was a deeply religious man she felt, so I agreed to see him.

I always sense a terrible impotence when I'm visiting someone seriously ill who has neglected the religious life; there is so little to talk about other than superficialities. Our actions, our manners, our words need the assurance of eternity, but lacking an inner conviction on the part of visitor or visitee, what we have to share often comes out weak or presumptuous or trite.

I entered his room to find him in a wheelchair. His head was shaved; a scar evident; he was on his way to physical therapy. He was depressed but lucid and in a hurry. I introduced myself. He seemed to know who I was. I told him his wife had asked me to come. I said, "I understand you're going through a pretty rough time."

He looked at his feet in the chair and said, "I just hope I can spare my wife a little. She works, so that's why I'm here."

"It must be rough on her with two kids, holding down a job," I replied.

"Yes, it is, but you'll have to excuse me, I'm late for therapy."

"Listen, I know you're hurried right now and have been through a lot, but would you like me to come again? . . . Is there anything you would like me to do for you?"

For the first time he looked at me. He had deep dark eyes. His face was gaunt and drawn; his body thin and nervous; but with his voice clear and distinct he said, "Yes, you can give me back the faith I had as a child."

He turned and wheeled himself out of the room.

I did return a number of times. He lived about a month after that, mostly not communicating at all. I will never forget his words to me. They were the last he ever spoke about his faith in spite of my efforts to renew the subject with him.

It made me think, How had the church prepared this man for that last year of his life? Oh, I know, he largely had himself to blame. Like most, he had other things to do. He had a wife that discouraged his churchgoing. But even if he had gone, would he have grown as a man? Would he have received enough spiritual food to strengthen him and help him through his last days? What would he find if he had come to our church? A sermon on Vietnam, Mai Lai, or Lieutenant Calley? Oh, there was more to us than that, but not much to grab on to and live for.

And what could I offer the man at that moment? I realized I couldn't give him faith anymore than I could give him a new brain. What inner strength did I have to even permit me to talk about faith with a dying man? I realized then that I simply had to do something about my inner life. I began to search for people to learn from.

I had contact with a few people who thought church a wonderful thing so long as you didn't take it too seriously. For them, church suppers, couples clubs, and circle meetings that didn't get too pushy about anything religious were just fine. Somehow they worked it out so that Christianity was the equivalent of respectability, niceness, moderation, and neatness. I wasn't sure which would be worse for them, to have their son come home and tell them he had given his life to Jesus or to have an unmarried daughter come home to announce her pregnancy. Fortunately, not many people fell into this sect.

Occasionally a more militant Christian would drop in on us. At first this Christian would seem to be caught up in an ecstasy that suggested the woman of Bethany. But it didn't take long to see their neuroses and self-righteousness. They spoke in tongues and were terribly judgmental of churches. They counted the number of times you mentioned Christ in a sermon, and if it wasn't enough, they were convinced you led people to hell and beyond. They formed a Christian AA group because Christ wasn't mentioned at conventional meetings, in spite of the fact that if Christ could have attended an AA meeting, he would have admired how Christian it was. Placing God at the center of their sobriety, they demonstrated in vivid color with their personal stories the Christian experience from death to resurrection. I must confess this type of Christian angered me the most. I considered them the demonic side of the Kingdom. They seemed to be, as Paul once remarked, the "spiritual forces of evil in the heavenly realms" (Ephesians 4:12).

But I also discovered Christian people who fell into a category that might be called the mountain movers. They would have literally interpreted Jesus' remark, "Have faith in God. . . . I tell you the truth, if anyone says to this mountain, 'Go, throw yourself into the sea,' and does not doubt in his heart but believes that what he says will happen, it will be done for him."[14] I had a tremendous admiration for this type of Christian even though at times they were the most difficult to understand. I was far too aware of the tragic in life; I was constantly haunted by a sense of futility fostered by the despair and worry that our near-comic commitments to powerless things bring to all of us. I was too conscious of the recurring fear we all have of death, disease, and surgical mutilation to believe that life could be so simply unburdened and manageable through the rose-colored glasses of faith. Yet at the same time I admired their positive feelings immensely. I had much to learn from their eagerness to see the benefits, the virtues, the hopes, and the hidden joys that up to now I had usually missed.

Still, they could be exasperating and insensitive. Much later, Joey became seriously ill. She exhibited an incredible faith, but also at moments quite normally experienced depression, fear, and dread. The typical answer from the mountain movers to the days when the demons of death assembled in her mind was "But you've got to have faith." What a belittling insensitivity to her faith that was. Much better to hold hands, to say, "It must be tough," or "I can't imagine what you're going through," or to say nothing at all—at least that allows a person the right to despair even as a member of the Kingdom. Certainly Jesus despaired at the sight of Jerusalem[15] and at the thought of the cross.[16]

A typical mountain-mover story was told to me by a church member. He said he was visiting another church one Sunday. It was pouring rain. In fact, it had rained all week, and still the deluge came. Cellars were flooded; sewers overflowed; people were being forced out of low-lying areas. After the service he turned to an unknown fellow worshiper and remarked, "Isn't it a terrible day!"

With a slight hesitation, the believer smiled and said, "Oh, no! It's a beautiful day the Lord has given us!" making him feel small, inadequate as a Christian, inferior for his negative thoughts.

Well, I rightly or wrongly categorized Christians. And I still felt at sea without any clear direction. As a person, I failed in niceness for most of my life. I would never be a very good master of ceremonies. I still had much to learn about how to be considerate, say the right things, back slap, shake hands, and be the friendly, unflappable, lovable pastor.

So I floundered and flapped. Self-pityingly I began to see that I had spent my life talking about things that failed to enrich a person's soul or inner capacity to cope with a tragic world. I desperately needed to grow in my own spiritual life. I couldn't possibly deal with the pain in people's lives unless I could bring to it an inner strength of my own that I didn't have.

I happened to read of Thomas Merton's journey in his book, *Seven Storey Mountain*. At one point he wrote, "They [the searchers] will find someone who is capable of telling them of the love of God in a language that will no longer sound hackneyed or crazy, but with authority and conviction: the conviction born of sanctity."[17] I knew Merton was right. I also knew that like Le Carre's spy I, too, had been out in the cold.[18] I had failed to develop a spiritual warmth that identified a genuine personal devotion to prayer, worship, and the Scriptures.

I had grasped at secular straws by joining organizations that fought for the poor, elderly, and minorities. And while I remain loyal to all these causes today, I couldn't avoid seeing an appalling lack of spiritual inspiration. It is that inspiration that, for the Christian at least, should have been the special stamp of faith in all of these issues.

But it has always been my experience that the Lord rarely fails to give us events to encourage the shreds and sparks of faith we already do have. In my case, Joey and I visited friends in Vermont and went to church with them on New Year's Eve.

The incredible cold forced us to keep flapping our arms and dancing in the snow to the tune set for us by a thermometer at twenty degrees below zero. The stars never shine so brightly as they do at that temperature, possibly because they seem to be the only warm thing available. The snow spoke with a sound that warned us of the cold as our feet crunched their way to a little monastery at the top of a hill. Warmth threw its arms about us as we entered the tiny chapel where the monks met for worship. The place almost yielded itself to us as if it were some kindly concierge with warm soup and bed urging us to stay the night. The radiance we felt was due partly to the physical warmth that met us at the door, but it was also a result of the spiritual patina of a thousand prayers and songs and communions that had been said, sung, and celebrated in that room. It piqued our imaginations and cheered our dispositions.

We crowded into the chancel around the table with a couple of monks and an assortment of people in bright ski clothes. Children, tourists, town folk, old, and young all seemed to hunger for what the monks prepared to give us. I had crunched up the hill with few expectations. My last experience at Mass on New Year's Eve twenty years before was one of drunkenness and boredom. Now, it was as if everyone in that tiny space expectantly craved spiritual food. A child, awed by being so near to the host and just tall enough to peer over the edge of the altar, watched with eyes full of wonder as if the celebrant were preparing a banana split. The monks spoke the familiar words of the invitation and communion. They sang the Sanctus, "Holy, Holy, Holy is the Lord of Hosts. . . ." Some familiar with the tune joined in. The beauty of the music filled that little place with a charm that made everyone's expression seem holy, hopeful, and radiant. The heavy clothing began to make itself known with the damp smell of sweat; snow melted off boots, shoes, and legs; but with our attention so securely riveted on the preparation, our physical condition didn't seem to matter. As I drank from the cup I sensed an overwhelming sensation of belonging, of joy and peace. At the kiss of peace we had held hands, then embraced one another; at the conclusion of the Mass we did the same all over again.

I left reluctantly, realizing we had been in the presence of the Holy Lord of Hosts, so much so that for a few brief moments everyone who crowded around the table was holy as well. I vowed to remember *that* communion for the rest of my life as we rode home in the quiet Vermont cold. I made a resolution to pursue the quality that I had found there, forever.

Since then I have learned there is a quality available in every experience, although it is an ingredient that is always elusive. We usually miss the potency of life because we are unprepared to accept it, believe in it, want it, or be patient enough to receive it. A commonplace episode of childhood will always remind me that the quality of our experiences has very much to do with what we bring to them.

For a child, fishing with a grandfather is a special event in itself. My grandfather, a small balding man with finely cut features and a great handlebar mustache, claimed my respect and awe by his appearance alone. It would have never entered my head to treat him lightly. He took a friend and I fishing for snapper blues, a small but succulent fish usually caught off docks or quays. At first we caught plenty of blues, but as the morning neared the noon hour, our success diminished to the point of waiting for nearly an hour without a bite. We were about to quit when a man arrived, baited his hook, and threw his line in about thirty feet from us. He immediately caught fish. We restless boys stared at him in wonder and began to inch toward his position, thinking the place where he stood held more fish than the rest of the dock. We nearly fouled his line as we cast as close to him as possible. Then we heard a shout from grandfather telling us to leave the man alone. He scolded us for our impropriety and said, "Don't you know it's not where you're standing that counts? It's the quality of the bait. He has fresh minnows." The moral of the story: The measure of the experience is determined by what we bring to it.

So far I hadn't brought many spiritual qualities to my ministry. I lacked the fresh spirit of sanctity and devotion that Merton talked about. I knew I had to find the same spirit in our church life that we experienced in Vermont and read about in the incident at Bethany. For a time, like the cormorant, I shook and quivered and stirred up the waters around me, feeling unproductive, water-logged, and tired of trying to get airborne.

The congregation at Park Ridge had been more than open to me. I knew if I had any hope of experiencing a ministry blessed by the presence of Christ, I had to work it out there. Going elsewhere was unthinkable. I had heard too many horror stories from ministers serving other churches. One man in a clergy sharing session told us how the wife of an influential parishioner would come to his house with soup. He cried as he told us how terrible the soup was, and, he said, she would time her visit for the lunch hour and stay until he ate the whole dish. He feared the woman's importance in his congregation too much to pour the soup down the drain where it belonged. Nothing like that had ever happened to me in Park Ridge.

I knew it was part of God's plan for me to find the solutions according to my own personality. After all, God must have wanted my particular character; he hadn't brought me this far for nothing. Whatever the solution was, it had to be real, and it had to be honest.

Pilate said to him, "What is truth?"

————JOHN 18:38 (RSV)————

8

The Real World

Sometimes collection plates contain things besides money. All sorts of articles appear over the years; buttons, screws, nails, scraps of paper scribbled on by an impatient child wishing to be somewhere else. Once there appeared two three-dollar bills in an envelope. But the most common exception to hard cash are notes intended for the pastor. Sometimes they are quite complimentary; sometimes they request a visit to someone the writer thought needed a "kind word"; sometimes they complain about such deeply spiritual needs as the loudness of the organ or the lack of bulletins or the draft from the stained-glass window that needs releading. One note I will always remember because I could have written it myself twenty years earlier:

Mr. Pope:

Nothing you can say can make me or my sister believe in
your *God*. I have never seen him. I doubt if you have. It
would be appreciated if you'd call my mother and tell her
to stop forcing us to come to church.

Harry Jones

The note surprised me because he signed his name.
Critical notes usually come anonymously because that is
the author's way of feeling better about insecurities; any
possible reaction or retaliation would defeat the purpose.
But not this kid. This kid threw down the challenge. He
wanted proof. No nonsense; show me.

He was a child of the age. Soap commercials that
demonstrate a difference in whiteness or softness compared to a baby's bottom were his bag. He would be
smoking *True* cigarettes because people who did appeared in happy, lilting bliss on his television screen.
Religion for him was hearsay, vague suppositions, and
dull traditions. I knew how he thought about reality. I
had thought the same way. And to a large degree I still
did. I was instantly attracted to this kid.

I wrote him a letter suggesting we get together. In the
letter I reassured him I wasn't after his spiritual hide and
wondered why he based his judgments on sight. I had
never seen an electron, but I knew they existed; nor had I
ever seen a toothache, but I sure felt one. I said I
recognized I couldn't prove to him that I had felt God's
presence anymore than I could prove that I had felt a
toothache. He would simply have to take my word for it
even though he couldn't see either one.

I had fun answering the boy's card. I enjoyed it

because in those days I continued to approach things pretty much with a technical mind; what might be called a resourceful personality or an I'm-from-Missouri attitude. I had been trained to believe in the power of negative thinking. I avoided making foolish mistakes by questioning every scrap of evidence, redoing my calculations two or three times, refusing to accept anything on the basis of what it seemed to be. In short, I thrived on skepticism.

Now I suddenly found myself in an opposite world. Except for a few scholars, very few people really questioned anything. Some took great religious pride in not being the least bit unsure about doctrines, dogmas, and traditions. Positive thinking seemed to be the mantra of faith. "No one wants to hear your doubts; just tell them what you know," a seminary professor had told me. Since at the time I could easily contain what I *knew* in one sermon, I wondered if the congregation had the patience to hear the same thing fifty-two Sundays a year.

Yet there were skeptical thinkers in this world. I recall shortly after arriving and enrolling in my first Bible course, a kindly professor, concerned that my convictions would be shattered by his teachings, took me aside to prepare me for a critical study of the Scriptures. He said, "Now you have to understand you're in *graduate* school. Here we analyze, parse, critique, and question the Hebrew, the syntax, the intention of the writer. You may have had some pretty firm ideas about Scripture that you probably got from Sunday school, but don't be too upset if some of your perceptions get twisted and turned around a bit. We have to help you learn how to question and probe till you get to the root of the meaning."

He meant well, but he wasted his speech on the

wrong person. I simply had no rigid preconceptions about anything, and I would have been shocked if his course proved to be anything other than what he described.

My guess is that at times even he wished life were less critical, more tolerant, more sure—like the life of the person with no questions. Sometimes it would be nice if there were pat answers to questions that are forever surrounded by doubt. It would be nice if in spite of all the searching and analysis of our convictions, we discovered no chinks in the armor. If only, for instance, we really did have an infallible cookbook to follow, filled with recipes for every human ill—wouldn't it be nice. If the pain, injustice, selfishness, and petty childishness were cured by reading the tenth chapter, verses six through nineteen in the book of so-and-so, it would be wonderful. It would be nice for a change not to worry about someone challenging your beliefs and principles and frustrating your best intentions with different opinions on prayer, life after death, and God himself, among other things.

If only intangible truths were a little more concrete, it would be delightful. If love could be measured and we could plug a couple about to be married into a computer screen and see the exact quality of their affection— thus saving them forty years of unhappiness—it would be great. If grief could be overcome with a good dose of paregoric, the inhaling of marijuana, or electric-shock therapy, it would save a lot of pain-filled time. If only joy were more predictable. By carefully filling a prescription of three office parties, two ball games, and one trip to Hawaii, joy could be ours forever, life would be pleasant indeed. If only the talents of Picasso, Bjorn Borg, and

Ronald Reagan were measurable, and we didn't need to rely on endless contradictory reports from ten different sources, we could save ourselves embarrassment and a little money, and we might even sleep better at night. If only we had a potion that would help us appreciate a traffic jam, rejoice when hearing Elvis Presley, and enjoy riding on crowded subways, the charms of life would far exceed its frustrations. If only God were more plain and didn't keep getting out of focus because of some controversy, tragedy, or lingering doubt, even *he* could be so much more satisfying. If only all these things were true, life would be comfortable, secure, and enjoyable.

Wouldn't it be better if God hadn't designed things the way he did? Sometimes I pray, "Lord, when you first sat down at your drawing board, why didn't you make it a little easier? Why couldn't you have biased the human heart a little more toward the good? If only the shadows weren't quite so deep and foreboding, Lord!" I'm sure we all sometimes wish it were different and wonder why God worked it out the way he did.

When Disney World opened in Florida, the same thoughts struck me and I wrote the following prayer of confession for our bulletin:

> Lord, would the real world be better if Disney designed it instead of you?
>
> We confess that we often think so. We would much prefer it if pain, hardship, and human suffering were make-believe. Fantasyland would be better. So, *we* say.
>
> But, Lord, in your good judgment, you made it different. Help us to believe your wisdom is greater than Disney's. Help us to believe your world is every bit worth living for with the help of Jesus, who thought it worth dying for . . . so we pray, in Christ's name. Amen.

In *Brave New World*, Aldous Huxley creates an imaginary land where pain and trouble and struggle are unknown.

> "It's Christianity without tears," describes the Controller.
>
> "But," someone says, "the tears are necessary. You get rid of them. You just abolish the slings and arrows. It's too easy. I don't want comfort. I want God. I want poetry. I want real danger. I want freedom."
>
> "But you'll be very unhappy," says the Controller.
>
> "I claim the right to be unhappy," replies the other.[19]

Well, I would agree with the man. For me, Christ gave me poetry, risk, and the freedom from grinding, impoverished selfishness; and now I can't imagine a life without these ingredients. In fact, can there be any joy without pain, doubt, or risk? Do the shadows add an essential outline to make the highlights in the painting recognizable? Does doubt have the positive quality of stimulating the search for truth, or more importantly, does it yield a deeper joy when conviction is achieved? Aren't the uncertainties far more exciting than what we know? Getting to the moon is exciting; the formula for calculating the thrust of a rocket engine would never make the headlines. And do the mountains in our way stimulate adventure, determination, achievement, and joy? And are the tears, to some degree, a measure of our blessings? The more priceless the treasure, the greater the grief when it is lost. The deeper the love, the more vulnerable we become. The more exceptional the relationship, the more tragic the separation. If paradise were a place without such things as risk, tears, and uncertainties, could it possibly contain contentment, gratification, rapture? Given the human qualities we have, paradise without pain would be a very selfish existence, which makes it all seem so un-Christlike to want to be there. No challenge, no risk, no danger, no judgment. Happiness is not being in some trouble-free welfare state. It's being with Christ.

I think we all really know deep inside that this is the best possible world—we just wish life could be a rose garden once in a while. One day our church secretary, Gail, seemed edgy. I had given her a lot of work; the phone had been ringing incessantly; and she had been often interrupted by people coming in and out of the office. I noticed her impatience and said in my best fatherly, ministerial manner, "Now we should be grateful to God for all these little frustrations. They are gifts he sends us to toughen us up for the bigger struggles and challenges. By testing our patience in little ways, he conditions us for the important battles ahead of us."

Just then the phone rang again. She looked at me in disgust and said, "Maybe this is one of God's little gifts for you." Then we both laughed.

But in that humor was the truth that though we wish it were easier, we know deeply there is probably no other way the world could be made.

Beyond this deep feeling, we know that the world we have makes Christ's achievement even more awesome. We look at great men in history, and while we admire them, we see that their greatness was achievable greatness. We can visualize their genius in the context of their humanity—their selfishness, egotism, indifference, arrogance—that colors even their exceptional parts with a human and fallible quality. But when we look at Christ, we are immediately humbled, knowing that his greatness is not achievable by any human means. To imagine that he stood under the same stars as we do; drank the same wines; felt the same gnawing temptations to bitterness, despair, and greed; struggled with the same evils; endured the same disappointments; felt the same desires and pleasures; and yet conquered sin—this remains an astonishing feat that, when we contemplate it, drives us to our knees.

So I continued to try to understand a reality not based on mathematical principles, a reality I had previously never considered to be reality at all. Someone once said that our poets would someday come to the rescue of our engineers. That certainly seemed possible, yet I remained uncomfortable in a world where the tangible goals were rarely achieved except for building churches and parking lots. I had been through one church building program as a layman only to discover bricks and mortar didn't do much for my spiritual life. Aside from this sort of thing, religion most often includes achievements whose meaning and durability have no immediate test, which is why I devoted many of my early days to more tangible projects like mental health, fair housing, the peace movement, civil rights, and why I spent a lot of time with teenagers. I could identify with them because they had the same religious skepticism I had grown up with.

I recall once in the sixties going on an overnight hike in the New Jersey hills near the Delaware Water Gap. These particular kids were highly intelligent and vocal nonbelievers. They had a vague church connection through friends and half-hearted parents. As we sat around the fire that evening, they spoke of the usual doubts about the miracles, the Bible, the virgin birth. We talked about the necessity of making a commitment to Christ in spite of doubts. I told them they were looking for the wrong kind of evidence. I said the experience of falling in love is what makes the doubts tolerable and acceptable. I said they needed to fall in love with Christ. If they did, the heavy questions would either be resolved or wouldn't matter anymore.

Well, I didn't get very far. I felt a little like Paul on Mars Hill delivering a sermon to ears attuned to more logical propositions.[20] The fire died down. Naturally, we were exhausted. (I was, at any rate—I felt as if I were a hundred years old, climbing over rocks all day, stumbling over roots, and jumping across streams.) I went to sleep quickly about ten o'clock.

I'm not sure whether those kids slept at all that night, but about four in the morning, they woke me excitedly. They were certain they were seeing strange UFOs landing in the distance. I groped my way out of my sleeping bag, found my shoes, and painfully staggered to the top of a hill where the others were staring off into the darkness. During the night a heavy fog had moved into the valley below us. They said they hadn't seen any thing for quite awhile, but several assured me that strange beings had settled into the valley below. Unhappily I sat down on a rock and waited, shivering in the damp night air.

As I sat there I gradually became aware of their conviction that some strange extraterrestrial phenomenon had slithered into the valley during the night. They actually seemed frightened, all huddled together in the dark and holding on to one another as if some spaceship would at any moment carry them off to a distant star.

And I felt myself getting angry not for being awakened but because I suddenly thought, What makes it so easy for these kids to believe there are UFOs skimming along under their stubborn noses and so hard for them to accept the virgin birth, the Resurrection, or Christ himself for that matter? Wasn't there a lot more hard evidence for the Christian faith than for UFOs? Hadn't there been initially skeptical observers who later witnessed with conviction about the Christ who appeared to them in a room with the doors shut?[21] Don't we have the words of those who saw and touched and heard Christ?[22] Don't we have evidence in our own hearts, somewhere in our subjective consciousness, that an element of love or truth or tenderness exists quite apart from what things seem to be like most of the time?

Well, I wanted to tell them all these things but couldn't. I couldn't because I knew they weren't ready to receive the gift of faith; maybe it was just as well not to force it on them to the point where they would have to reject it and spend the rest of their lives living up to their denial. In fact, maybe there are times when God will not force us into a course that is irreversible or lead us into some decision we will never live down—the entropy of a lost moment, of opportunity not lost in circumstance but in conviction, in mindset, in stubbornness.

Sometimes we spend a lifetime proving our negative convictions as much as our positive ones. We decide in high school that there is no practical reason for studying Shakespeare; a poor teacher convinces us that we'll never be able to add a column of figures; on some religious retreat, we are forced to deny Christ, for whatever reason—embarrassment, faddishness, childish foolishness. How many inner beliefs about ourselves, about reality, about others do we spend a lifetime living up to, missing Shakespeare or a hidden talent or the touch of the living God? What errors do we convince ourselves of? What beliefs about ourselves do we program for failure in order to prove our convictions right? What exciting pastures do we miss seeing because we have never trained our eyes to see them?

These kids were seeing something that I didn't see, so maybe I had missed something too. I sat peering into the blackness and dampness until the rock I perched on had nearly paralyzed my posterior. I had seen nothing but an occasional automobile headlight drifting through the fog-bound valley. Unwilling to sacrifice any more sleep for the sake of curiosity, I rolled up in my sleeping bag a second time, feeling inadequate and angry with my own inept example of faith and with their obstinate unbelief.

For a long time after that sleepless night overlooking the Delaware River Valley, I struggled with my perceptions of reality. I realized how elusive spiritual experiences had been in my life. I did see through the glass darkly, because I allowed myself to be programmed to think and act in concrete ways. Before I went to seminary I never took a course or lifted a book or read a story unless it had some practical consequence. I had a master's degree from Columbia University, but I had never written a term paper. The lab report, the analytical study, the statistical essay were my highest literary achievements. I knew instantly what was practical, and it hadn't occurred to me there could be any use for experiences that would strengthen character, enrich the inner man, deepen the soul, or enlarge one's empathic horizons.

I realized I had been goal oriented. The irony was that many of the religious journals were pushing goal setting as an incredible new idea guaranteed to move the church ahead. Right then, I struggled desperately to catch some sense of the now, the moment, the immediate, and to a degree learn how to disconnect myself from the endless goals I set for myself. We live in one time frame only—the present. I knew I had become so future-programmed that I couldn't enjoy the present at all. Besides, didn't God come in the moment? Of course, he is always coming, but if all our moments are spent in a frenzy—mere stepping stones to our achievements—I would never discover Christ again.

In spite of all my coming and going, my protests and actions, my social preaching and exaltation of youth, my pleading and urging others to action, God seemed to inch me toward an inner reassessment. I knew I needed more than programs to offer people. I knew I needed more than causes to follow. I knew I couldn't deal with the troubles and difficulties people endured unless I could offer them some kind of inner sanctity. I knew I had been given a great gift—the unimaginable gift of new life. I had been turned away from the pit, resorted, redirected. O.K., now where Lord?

Suddenly the thought struck me: "Would I . . . could I be in danger of losing this gift of faith?" So far, I remained within the divine grasp. I may have strayed; I may have ignored and denied my faith through my failures to live as I should, but a holy scent haunted me. The hound of heaven ceaselessly and relentlessly ran at my heels. I had never lost the conviction that God continued to hold me in his grasp. I still had, as they say, a blessed assurance.

This confidence is like setting out on an unknown trail with gnawing fears of getting lost, of not finding water, of not finding a warm protected place to sleep at night, but having a trail map and compass in your pack.

It's like living in a place where thieves break in. You may worry about having your goods stolen, but at the same time you have an insurance policy in the drawer.

It's like being alone during the cold, frozen days of winter, hearing the lonely whistle of the pines—endless winter days, depressing, drab, dull, and bone-cold—but then knowing that spring is certain and that underneath the snow lie the seeds that contain each flower and petal and blossom.

It's like having someone love you. Like the best of relationships, it's often filled with tensions, misunder-standings, even hurts due to prideful, unthinking, selfish, irresponsible actions; yet you know that beneath it all lies a lover. Such confidence is built on years of working the problems out, years of forgiving and being forgiven, years of coming back to each other with peace in your heart.

A terror now seemed to grow within that I might lose this gift. Gifts were easily lost if ignored. Faith, someone suggested, isn't like eating: The less you eat the more you hunger and the more you want food. Faith is just the opposite: The less you practice faith, the less you hunger for it and want it.

I remember one of the happiest days of my life as a boy. We didn't have much as kids. My father worked during the depression, but we struggled at keeping things together. One unforgettable summer afternoon my father pulled into the driveway with a new bicycle in the back of his car. To this day I don't know what the occasion was; it wasn't my birthday or anything, and I was too young to ask about the motive for his generosity (or too overwhelmed to think of asking). But what a wonderful gift.

My only problem—I didn't know how to ride a two-wheeler. We never heard of training wheels in those days; my guess is they would have been for sissies in our world. You learned to ride a bike by falling off. You got on next to a bank or a wall. You were too small to swing your leg over it since the economy demanded you buy a bike bigger than you could comfortably handle. You practiced by wobbling down the street until you fell off or crashed into the ditch. Soon I discovered the more I practiced, the better I got, until one day I could go no-hands around a corner. That bike was a great gift that I could have become discouraged about, put in the garage, and never learned to ride until a broken-hearted father sold it or gave it to someone else. In that way, all gifts are the same, whether they be bicycles or faith.

I did grow up and eventually put the bike in the garage. Now occasionally I ride my daughter's bike, but my whole body screams out because I've neglected exercising it. I come away from my escapades with a springy feeling in my knees. Likewise we neglect the gift of faith at the peril of feeling that same weakness in the knees when we come face to face with our finitude or the tragedy of our human condition. Unless we treat the gift of faith with reverence, awe, and as pure gift, we will never "strengthen [our] feeble arms and weak knees" and "make level paths for [our] feet" (Hebrews 12:12, 13a).

I had been too busy with the journey outward to

consider the journey inward. The realization that I needed to consider a change in direction overwhelmed me.

As I read about the saints, a chief characteristic that I notice in their lives is their ability to live in the present. Good engineers are good planners and good learners. They plan toward some objective, learn from prior experience and from calculation. The present is a means toward an end and rarely an end in itself. But the only living we do is in the moment. I had to learn something about the "holy carelessness of the eternal now," as George Macdonald put it.[23] Or as Anne Morrow Lindbergh cried out in pleading prayer:

> God let me be conscious of it! Let me be conscious of what is happening *while* it is happening. Let me realize it and feel it vividly. Let not the consciousness of the event (as happens so often) come to me tardily, so that I half miss the experience. Let me be conscious of it!

How many experiences had I already lived *through* and had not lived *in*. God is available in the now, and so far, I had lived in the hope of finding him in accomplishments, in a petition, a cease-fire, a well-used building, a basketball court. I imagined him always ahead of me, and as hard as I ran, planned, and aspired, he seemed to run harder. He seemed like the cloud by day and the pillar of fire by night, leading and out of the reach of the people of God (Exodus 13:21–22); I seemed always expectant, never meeting, knowing, or experiencing him. I hungered for righteousness, and all my busy committees, programs, plans, and schemes lacked the quality I sought and couldn't define. Life had been a grasping, gorging, feverish affair.

I wonder at my dog. I give him a morsel, a piece of steak, and it drops like a stone to his stomach. Why doesn't he savor it, roll it around in his mouth, enjoy the moment by getting every bit of flavor out of it before he swallows it? I suppose it's because he wants to be ready for the next piece. Out of pure anticipation and gusto he misses the moment's supreme taste. Yet I did the same thing. I bit off life in chunks, ravenously anticipating what was to come, never meeting the moment or pausing to taste the refreshing flavor of what I was doing at the moment.

Even when I had a day off and was supposed to be free, I enslaved myself to a program, schedule, or goal. I would wake in the morning and immediately plan the day. While I shaved I began to make a mental list— there's leaves that need raking; the dog has to go to the vet for a shot; if I don't get the plants out of the ground and into the window greenhouse, the frost will get them; the garden needs to be cleared; the garage is a mess; the cellar needs to be straightened; a trip to the dump would be a good idea.

While I ate breakfast I began to organize the tasks in my mind. Let's see, I don't want to make too many trips in the car; gas is too expensive. Maybe I had better clean the cellar first, then I can load up the car for the dump including the dog so I can go right there from the vet. On the other hand, the weatherman said something about rain this afternoon, so maybe the first thing to do is rake the leaves. So before breakfast I began to find tension building about getting everything done. I gulped down my coffee, avoided a lengthy conversation with my wife, and dashed out the door. I simply needed to do *something* that would let me pause long enough to let peace enter my life.

I am now convinced the reason we do not know God is we don't know how to look for him while things are happening. We expect some miracle, some mighty act in time of desperation, some healing, some special reprieve from sadness, but rarely does that happen. As I look back over my life I see that the special moments were much more ordinary and immediate than I realized. I see them as the times we ate together as a family, the periods of digging in my garden, the calls I made on lonely or hurting people, the rare wedding when a bride and groom had a quality that promised to us all a great hope, the fragments of conversation that expressed warmth and honesty and joy, the bits and pieces of life that always seemed to center on common, everyday experiences. All these things seemed to be suddenly precious and God-filled.

Alistair Cooke tells a story told to him by Adlai Stevenson about the night Stevenson spent in the White House as a guest of Harry Truman. Stevenson had recently lost the 1952 election to Eisenhower. He was put in the Lincoln Room. When he got ready for bed, he looked at the bed and shuffled around it in awe. But he couldn't bring himself to lie in it. He spent the night on the sofa instead.

Cooke says he doesn't know whether Stevenson was ever apprised of the irony, but in Lincoln's day the bed wasn't there and the sofa was.[24]

I like that story because it's so true of life. We are forever appraising things, shuffling around them with reverence and awe—a grand home, a trip to some exotic place, a beautiful car—only to discover they are not sacred at all. Yet when we look back on life, to our surprise it's the ordinary sofas we've bedded down in that are special; the ordinary turns in our lives to do this instead of that; the brief moments when we've felt warm, secure, and loved; the laughter of the children; the eating together; the dreaming together—these things have been sacred.

I like what Paul Sherer says of Jesus; Jesus could take ordinary, mundane experiences and breathe a time-lessness, a loveliness, a profundity into them. Sherer writes that the gospel is

> just a heaped-up mass of little things that you and I want to get by somehow. They seem to lie so heavily on us, make us fretful and impatient: and the sum of them is life! A carpenter's bench, a lake, a highway, and a hill. Homes where death has been, and the blinds drawn. A wedding, a supper, and a woman by a well. Men fishing and sowing and building and reaping. People in pain. A father who has lost his boy, and wanders out at evening time to watch for him down the long shadows. That is the stuff God took up in his hands. And we brush it off, and say that we're sick of it, and that none of it amounts to anything! Why doesn't he give us something that's really worthy of us, and not this tiresome rubbish that takes up all our time? And God made Jesus out of it . . . out of common days like ours![25]

I knew I had missed the truth about God; he is as near as the air I breathe. He's in the hospital lobby as I stop to speak to the guard about his family. He's near me as I dig my fingers into the earth and feel its tilth and richness. He's there as I come in from the cold morning walk and my wife has the coffee ready for breakfast. He's

there in the fear I see in a woman's eyes the night before
she submits to surgery to explore a lump in her breast.

But most of my days I had spent missing God. It
occurred to me that to a degree *I* remained lost. I had
tried to be a pastor without inner spiritual integrity. I
could as easily have been a social worker, a counselor, a
manager, an administrator, or an organizer at General
Motors or Best Foods, and it wouldn't have been any less
Christian than what I had been doing.

Later, while spending a few days in a continuing-
education course at Princeton Seminary, I happened to
be browsing in the book store, and I picked up Brother
Lawrence's *The Practice of the Presence of God*,[26] a thin,
deceptively simple little volume. For me it turned out to
be a book of great importance. Out of its pages emerged a
simplicity and marvelous contentment. It told of a man
who had spent thirty years in the scullery of a monastery
and had such a serene countenance that even bishops
and cardinals became interested in his accomplishments
among his pots and pans. One line, overpowering in its
plainness, was the source of a blessing and a power I had
not known before. Brother Lawrence urges "that we
should feel and nourish our souls with high notions of
God; which would yield us great joy in being devoted to
him." As I repeat this sentence it seems almost silly to
make anything out of it. Approaching it intellectually or
philosophically produces no new insight at all. "High
notions of God" that yield some profound cosmic theory
or mind-challenging volume had already been achieved,
and while they clearly had their place, they failed to
produce any contentment other than feelings of accomplishment for their mastery.

The profundity of Brother Lawrence's words lies in

the special impact of all his conversations and letters. They might better be labeled a handbook, a working instruction book for putting faith into practice. It suddenly struck me that all the books I had read on prayer had dealt with the theory of prayer, the meaning of prayer, the explanation of prayer. No wonder they had no impact. They attempted to satisfy my mental objections, never invading my life—my heart—with the presence of God. I needed books that spoke of prayer in practical ways. I needed how-to books. I didn't need prayer *explained*; I needed prayer projected in *workable* forms.

With great anticipation and hunger I began to read the mystics, men and women who lived out their lives with God in practical ways. I read *The Imitation of Christ, The Cloud of Unknowing, The Way of a Pilgrim, Introduction to the Devout Life, The Search for Silence,* to name a few.[27] I began to practice Brother Lawrence's method of "nourishing myself with high notions of God."[28] I found that by spending a half hour each morning deliberately putting myself in the presence of God—letting the wandering thoughts and tensions drift away from my consciousness so as to reach the point where I sensed a presence, a truth, a reality—I would experience an inner joy and peace that overwhelmed my senses. I knew a *presence*. The silence became pregnant, rich with meaning, and, as Brother Lawrence puts it, contained "inward motions so charming and delicious that I am ashamed to mention them."[29]

It was during or after this joy that I would bring my petitions before God. I would allow the faces of those for whom I prayed to move into his presence. I didn't ask for anything for them, except that God would care for them in his own way and in his own time.

I had questions. I wondered if I might be deluding myself or experiencing some psychological quirk or turn-on. Yet my reading reassured me that others across the expanse of Christian history had had similar experiences. I've been at it five years. I rarely let a day go by without a daily attempt to put myself, and those who have special needs, in God's care. I say attempt because sometimes I get in the way; my wandering thoughts are uncontrollable; some overwhelming concern will not leave my mind; or for some inexplicable reason I'm simply unable to settle down to the point where God can reach me. Now I'm hooked. I look forward to the time each day when I can simply offer God my life as it is with all its inner tensions and outward worries. I find a peace in those minutes that I have never experienced by any other means. I make prayer lists of people whose faces I bring before the Lord for his consideration, concern, and healing. I try to offer the Lord our human condition, our ignorant, blundering, misled, faltering good intentions, and let him soak down through our lives. This discipline has given me a new vantage point, a new understanding of the Christian life that I did not have before.

I'm a gardener. I grow vegetables. I used to think, "My, how poorly the Lord cares for my garden. All those weeds and rocks and poor soil. So he needs me to pull the weeds, clear the rocks, and enrich the earth. He waits for some farmer to come along before he can grow things. He needs a doer, a believer. Someone has to first believe food can be grown on that land, in that meadow, in that rock strewn pasture."

Now I see it differently. God imposes on his creation an energy for growth and increase. A powerful bias toward life exists. If it didn't, humankind couldn't have survived floods, dinosaurs, radiation showers, glaciers, and saber-tooth tigers. I love a picture one of our young people took of a flower growing up through a crack in the asphalt. There exists a certain tenacity for life. God breathes through his creation a positive influence, a grace, and an unexplainable presence. And to be successful at living we need to get in tune with that influence.

Gardeners merely arrange the soil to fit His growth system. Doctors learn how to apply medicines, X-rays, and therapies to allow healing to take place. Engineers devise techniques for taking advantage of physical laws so people can fly. The farmer doesn't cause growth; the doctor doesn't heal; the engineer doesn't fly. Likewise, the Christian doesn't pray. He allows God to pray through him by fulfilling the conditions for prayer. Prayer unveils the Presence already eager to become a reality. It is *God's* will that is done. Paul says, "We do not know what we ought to pray, but the Spirit himself intercedes for us with groans that words cannot express."[30] Prayer teaches me to allow God to intercede— to do his thing in my life and in the lives of others. In a sense, liberation occurs. I let God be the Messiah that I no longer have to be. What *I* do isn't crucial anymore. How willing I am to submit my plans and schemes to God's will and intentions becomes the key to success.

It no longer seemed necessary for me to prove myself or invent endless ways of changing people or make excuses for God. Let it be. Let it all be; and soon I discovered to my amazement his beauty and strength around me, especially in some quite unexpected people.

"I have many people in this city"

—Acts 18:10b—

9

God's People

I like children's puzzles where you search through a
line-drawing of woods or shrubbery or weed patches to
find faces and figures. You look and look, turning the
picture this way and that, searching for the ten faces that
are supposed to be there; you find six or seven, but the
rest remain hidden. More turning. You force your imagination to the page, searching every line for a familiar
shape or likeness. You put it down, thinking a fresh look
in an hour will do something to your eyes to adjust them
to the hidden forms. Then suddenly they leap out of the
page at you. In fact it becomes impossible to look at the
picture without seeing them. For some reason they
appear to your mind before the woods and you can no

longer lose them in the brambles. You wonder why it took so long for them to appear.

Sometimes life is like that. Familiar forms, ideas, and situations lull us into blindness. We fail to see the real personalities and faces available to us. People emerge on the surface in routine ways. Their depth and quality fail to enter the conscious mind until suddenly that myopia of our heart lifts and we appreciate something that has been there all along.

As an example, I think of Phil Bandstra. We hadn't seen him since the Billy Graham days. He happened to be in town one day at lunchtime, and he stopped by. We renewed our friendship and covered ground long since past—the status of our kids and jobs. He had a business partner now and owned a dry-cleaning store. He still laughed about his kids and his own impatience. But I began to see a Phil I hadn't really recognized before. I had generally pictured him a Dutch evangelical: a straight, formal type of personality who didn't deviate from prescribed Christian behavior. I had imagined he was one of those exclusive people who had been privy to the Lord's intentions, one who helped decide who got into the Kingdom. I had seen him as someone who was so sure of what a Christian ought to be like that I had developed an inner tension about myself whenever I thought of him. Instead of feeling relaxed and comfortable, I felt tense, on guard, and defensive. (That is what the self-righteous do to us.)

But now a different Phil had emerged, and I felt sorry I had missed him before. As is the custom in some circles, he brought us a bottle of wine when we invited him and Marge, his wife, to dinner. Wine! What other bones did he have in his closet? But what was more, I now saw a Christian who struggled with his own sin—a sign of the authenticity of his character. He told us of his impatience. He laughed beautifully at an episode in the hospital. He had gone in for tests for a heart condition. As he entered the hospital room the nurse told him to undress and get into bed. He refused. After all, it was midday and he felt fine; why should he get into his nightclothes and go to bed? He had the entire nursing staff in a frenzy, but he won out. He went to bed when it was time to do so, but not until after he had glared at every medical person who asked where "Mr. Bandstra" had gone when they came into the room and saw him sitting in the chair with his clothes on. He delighted in telling them where he wished Mr. Bandstra could have gone.

There is nothing so real as someone who isn't ashamed of their feelings. It's when we hide anger or impatience and pretend that we have no impurities that they poison us. I saw Phil, a man who had long since come to terms with his Lord, now coming to terms with himself. He knew in certain situations he could be caustic, harsh, cutting, and obstinate. Yet at the same time he knew the Lord loved him. Phil was one of those truly good people not because he had become perfect but precisely because in his imperfection he had become what God intended him to be.

I wrote him a note shortly after he had reappeared on our porch. I told him how important he had been to my spiritual journey. It is quite possible that except for him I would never have become a Christian. I supposed the Lord would have found some other way to bring me into his Kingdom, but I was immensely glad that he worked it out so that Phil would be the instrument of his grace for me. We both, I think, briefly warmed our hearts on each other's renewed friendship.

Then tragedy. Marge called to say he had been taken to the hospital in the night with chest pains. This time he went directly to intensive cardiac care, no arguments about going to bed. He lived for another two weeks. I saw him once during that time. I visited him with some misgivings. Knowing what well-meaning friends can do to you when you are very sick and they appear healthy and lighthearted, I cautiously entered his room. He recognized me, grabbed my hand, and said, "I've been to the brink." I held his hand and prayed with him. I sat for a few minutes, mostly in silence, and left his room. I never saw him again. His last words to me were, "Bob, you have made my day."

Phil's death helped me appreciate people and especially the gifts God has given them. I, more than any other person, knew he had been in God's plans. I'm absolutely sure he is in heaven, still getting angry, but still laughing at himself, still poring over the Scriptures to enlighten some lesser Christian soul on their meaning, and enjoying every minute of it.

I kept Phil's bottle of wine for quite a while. I cherished it. For me it took on an almost sacred significance. I couldn't help but think of the wine Jesus gave his disciples to remember him by. For them *His* incredible personality would forever be brought to mind when they shared a cup together. Now for me, too, when I shared Phil's bottle of wine with someone, it would be a special occasion indeed. I would see pictures and images of honesty, laughter, joy, and authenticity. Just as that wine reminded me of the personality of Phil, so I now could see more clearly why the cup of blessing contained the essence of our Lord. Since Phil's death, the eucharist would never be the same again. Jesus' gift to his disciples and us was that the drinking and eating together in his name enabled the participants to savor once more the personality, quality, and Spirit in remembrance and power.

Someone once said that the inability to love is merely a failure of imagination. Like the imperfect search we make of the child's line-drawing, we don't see the real faces of people that confront us, because our comprehension, our empathy, and our insight fails us. Church people are very much like the puzzle. We usually see their Sunday look. We see them on their best behavior and sometimes miss what makes them understandable. We miss the struggle that befits the façade, the piety, and the peculiar claim Christ has on them. It takes patience, time, and sometimes conflict to know a person, to see how a person fights or masks a particular corruption.

There are Christians, for instance, who seem to deny all that Christ would have them do, who are stingy in their relationships, easy to anger, quick to criticize. Yet when the puzzle fully reveals itself, we find persons who desperately want to live differently and sense that the answer lies in Christ. Or there is the parsimonious Christian, who is afraid something or someone will separate him from his money, but works out his avidity by giving his time to others, generously inconveniencing himself to help someone in trouble. Or then there is the sensitive Christian who, emotionally unable to take controversy, consistently avoids even the most worthy of Christian causes; yet in the contagion of that personality, this sensitive one becomes an enviable witness to the blessed assurance of faith in Christ.

We forget that most of us who claim Christ aren't much different than the disciples. They didn't know much about religion. They were fisherman, tax collectors, political malcontents, men who were making it, and men who were not. They came from mediocrity. Because of Christ they are remembered, not because *they* did anything. Many faded into legend and obscurity and would not be known except for a nondescript list appearing in the Gospels. Most misunderstood Jesus, had the wrong motivations, argued among themselves, and beat it when things got tough. Yet, for all this, Christ chose them, counted on them, and called them the Kingdom of God. And they became the bearers of grace for us if we only persist in looking again and again for the face of Christ that appears from the scanty accounts of their lives.

If I have grown as a Christian, as a man, and as a human being, it is because I've seen in ordinary church people moments of heroism. Often, in spite of their fear, intense struggle with sin, confusion mixed with anger and sympathy over the sins of the world, and flashes of self-denial, they reveal moments of intense belief. The amazing thing is that so many still come to church in spite of how the world has misled them and hurt them. We grow when we know what goes on in a man or woman, and usually when we know the full story, we can't help but be awed by their strength, sincerity, and belief. It is a humbling experience to see how people have kept their faith, their sanity, and their hope.

I recall, for instance, Jenny and Lodi, a couple in

their seventies, who had continued living in a house with a cast-iron oil stove in the kitchen. They saved every newspaper and magazine they ever bought. I had been warned before I went to Park Ridge that Jenny would drop in for prayer at every opportunity. A nearby colleague called me to tell me how embarrassing she could be, making you feel awkward and uncomfortable as she burst into your study, held your hand, and prayed for the pastor and his family.

But I grew to love Jenny. She never missed a church supper for miles around, and I understood why when I saw the newspapers stacked on her stove. They were always the first to arrive at church meetings, and they would often bring a butternut squash, tied with a red ribbon, for the pastor. Jenny loved the Lord, and though Lodi had spiritualist leanings—he often said he spoke to his spirit friends—he did too. They were a precious, eccentric couple who helped me see how effective simple faith could be. They had a cheerful contentment with ordinary things and with old age that most people should have envied. They helped me grow by letting me see how unadorned and credulous the Christian faith could be.

Then there was Irene, a woman in her nineties. She was a very proper woman who advised me to take the word "douches" out of the manuscript of my first book. But Irene was a tremendously creative and curious person. She wrote stories and articles to be read at Christmas or Easter at a ladies' circle meeting. She, in part, led me to the conviction that preachers need to learn how to be storytellers.

But above all she questioned. No blessed assurance for her. Pain and human sorrow threw God into question over and over again in her mind, and I appreciated her doubts about those who oversimplified the Christian faith. She was the opposite of Jenny (they were, in fact, distantly related). She always had a list of questions to ask me when I called, mostly questions I couldn't answer. She had a remarkable mind and understood reasons for unbelief that many of us preachers are guilty of treating in a cavalier fashion. So she kept my feet on the ground. I never drifted off into clichés and platitudes while she was around.

Elwood was an engineer in his fifties. I loved to hear him describe his technical problems, especially after he took a job at Jenkins Valve, a company I had worked for as a blueprint boy in high school. He made me realize how much I missed those exciting days and that technical world where we could rely on very practical answers to our difficulties. Elwood searched the Scriptures for anchors of belief as if he needed some divine reassurance. He never missed a Bible study when he wasn't traveling. It was as if he knew how much he would soon need every crumb of grace. After he and his family moved from our area, he would keep in touch by letter, often sending us items he made. We still have a tiny wooden cross, fashioned out of driftwood, over our mantle.

They discovered cancer in Elwood's intestine. He suffered a long, painful, and difficult illness. His wife, Carolyn, seemed to grow in faith because of it. I still have a letter she sent to a friend that revealed a tenderness and a belief I had yet to understand or experience.

> We are away on a holiday! Last March we took this cottage not knowing what was in store. I wondered, but here we are only about two hundred feet over a little dune

covered with sea oats. And there is the majestic Atlantic Ocean. I am writing to the rhythm of the waves on the beach. We are overwhelmed at God's goodness. Our life has come into sharp focus, and we find joy in little acts of love and simple beauty. We only have a toe hold on something real, mysterious, and exciting! God knows we have our ups and downs and we stumble, but he picks us up and on we go.

Much love goes out to you—we know these are sunset days—darkness is coming but then God will send us a star!

Elwood revealed a courage that I still consider with awe. He had been touched by something that is far beyond us.

And Tom. Tom was a high-school graduate who disliked the classroom and loved to run. By the time he finished high school, he had nine varsity letters in track. Not planning to go to college, he worked in the mailroom of an office building in Montvale, New Jersey. He seemed to be opening himself to a deeper Christian experience, so I invited him to go along with me and some others to a nationwide evangelism meeting in Detroit. At that meeting, Tom discovered Christ in a way that proved indispensable. Evangelist Tom Skinner awakened something in Tom. As he later wrote,

> I listened closely, and I felt something inside me wanting to jump out and say to everyone, "Did you hear what I heard from Skinner! Jesus is real—alive. Let's get off our asses and do something about racism and the barriers between people! We have Jesus Christ to lead us!" After Detroit I knew that Jesus Christ was real and was involved with me personally.

Tom didn't know at the time just how important that experience would be; two years later he broke his neck in a swimming accident at the Jersey shore. He was completely paralyzed from the neck down. If he hadn't been pulled from the water by a friend, he would have drowned.

As soon as I got the call that Tom had been hurt, I went to see him at Point Pleasant Hospital. The intensive-care unit was small and confining: six or eight beds crowded into a room full of nurses, machines, intravenous bottles, and flashing, beeping monitors. Tom lay flat on his back with a pair of tongs fastened to his skull and attached to weights that put tension on his back and spine. He didn't say much during that visit or, for that matter, during any of the visits over the next nine weeks. Fear, bewilderment, anger, tears, pain were to fill his days, months, years. Yet from the moment of injury, a miracle began to take place in Tom's life. The miracle had to do with a slow, painful, frustrating return of movement in his arms and a deepening and strengthening of faith.

Tom, a high-school jock who had prided himself in his athletic ability and had refused to consider anything academic beyond high school, came back and discovered abilities and strengths he didn't know existed. Tom went from the General Hospital at Point Pleasant to the Kessler Institute for Rehabilitation where he remained another eleven months. At that time he wrote the following:

> I ran track for four years, and during that time I learned a few things. To win the race your body has to be in the best of shape in order to take the wear and tear to beat your opponent. Not only does your body have to be in shape, but your attitude does as well. That will decide the

outcome of whether you win or lose. Also, for the team to win, each person has to pull for the other.

Being in the state that I and my roommates are, we find that our condition is the same as that of a track team. We have to have the same spirit that is needed to win a race. In Room 176 we have the kind of spirit that will pull us through. When one hurts we don't cry about it, but we give the person the will power to fight whatever hurts (at least we try and it usually helps). We realize that to be able to walk again, we have to be ready to endure pain.

I must admit there are times when my two roommates noticed my pain and what they said was "come on, Tom, you can take it." And just hearing those words, I knew that they also were feeling my pain. Another great asset about being with such great people is the laughter that goes on. When we can laugh about things and not feel down because of our accidents, then I know we'll make it. *It's when you always feel sorry for yourself that you lose.**

In our room we are open to each other, and when one tends to get upset, we straighten him out for his own good. And believe me that becomes necessary many times. Sometimes it hurts to know the truth about yourself, but it pays off in the long run.

There's another thing about our room I'd like to mention, that's our faith in God. With that kind of faith behind us, we know we can't lose.

I'm not saying that because we have faith that everything is all roses. It's not. But with the faith we have, and the kind of roommates I have, we are going to walk again.

Tom returned home more a year after he had happily set out to spend a day at the shore. Tom never walked

---

*Italics mine.

again, but he is a miracle nevertheless. He learned to drive a specially equipped car. He went to Ramapo College and earned a degree in sociology. He works everyday for the disabled and has made a significant contribution toward a proposal for independent living for the handicapped that our church is privileged to participate in.

Tom's story inspires all of us because he has surmounted incredible odds. He triumphed over his attitudes. He did not let the cruelty of life hammer him to death. Instead, he has been the anvil on which the hammer has shattered. What happened to him unveiled a strength even he didn't know he had. By God's grace he wasn't allowed to cling to what was less than himself. At one point during the rehabilitation process he wrote:

> I still have moments of anger, depression, and uncertainty—all of us do. But I believe that I have become stronger in my faith.
>
> I know there are hard times facing me in the future. Because you believe in Christ does not mean everything is going to be like a rose garden. There will be many experiences for me in life in which I will grow from—some good, some bad.
>
> No one, I believe, who says they know Jesus can ever think they have found everything there is to know about life—about living. Christianity is a growing process. I want to live life—to share what Christ has taught me—and not merely exist.

Tom revealed the tremendous asset of faith. Of course, none of us could predict what would have been the result if Tom had not gone to Detroit. We do know that life can defeat us or inspire us. In Tom's case tragedy found a resourcefulness, a determination, a tenacity that was far from evident on graduation day one fine June evening. The difference between the moment he stepped forward for his diploma and the time of the accident was an evangelist by the name of Tom Skinner through whom a new ingredient—a morsel of grace—began to nourish Tom's soul in a way that would prove indispensable to his recovery.

Tom, more than anyone, inspired me to never lose sight of the power of God, not so much in its ability to change things or make them beautiful as in its ability to see us through even unto death. Later, as you will see, Joey and I would experience firsthand the same power that enriched and restored Tom's life. Grace often comes in what we suppose are fleeting, irrelevant moments, but those moments prepare us for incredible gifts of strength. In the midst of whatever life brings to us, there rises up like a wellspring a stamina and a grit. We stand in awe and wonder at the power that is available to move us to praise and worship and to experience the never-ending conviction of his love.

Of course, many others shared in my growing up. It's impossible to tell about them all. Some I cannot write about without violating confidence and trust. But I learned that God uses people—people to love us, yes. But more than that God uses people who through their troubles inspire within us convictions that can sustain us even in our poorest moments. Someone said we live in a world that we can hardly embrace with any enthusiasm. True. But the creator hasn't left us on a planet of hopelessness. He shares our dejection, pain, bewilderment, separation. And for that reason, we claim him as our own.

*"When you pass through the waters,
I will be with you;
and when you pass through the rivers,
they will not sweep over you.
When you walk through the fire,
you will not be burned;
the flames will not set you ablaze."*

———Isaiah 43:2———

10

Grace Revisited

During a ministerial gathering, one of the men spoke
movingly about his lost son. He said he and his wife
considered their children gifts from God, on loan, so to
speak. God intended they be cared for, encouraged on
their journey, disciplined if need be, taught Christ's way,
and always loved. He and his son, he felt, had respect for
one another. Though not often acquainted with each
other's inner murmurings and reflections, they did have
the affection that somehow endured the mutual disillu-
sionments that inevitably occur as a child grows to
maturity.

With a steady and unwavering voice he described
how he drove his son to Newark Airport for the last time.
His destination, Vietnam. Together they found the depar-

ture gate, and as they approached the metal detector beyond which the father could not go, his son turned to him and said, "Dad, don't worry about me. I feel right with men, and I'm okay with God." Two weeks later his son, a strong Dutch tower of manhood, was dead.

Reflecting on the grief he and his wife experienced, he meditated on the strange interrelationship of blessing and curse. He thought we could not have one without the other. "Because we were blessed much, we now grieve much," he said. He knew more than the words he said because as Christians, we are acutely aware of how much the predicament and redemption of life have to do with the cross.

The cross with all its sentimentalized and forgotten ugliness and pain takes on the paradox of blessing and curse. It represents these truths: Never having risked much, one will not lose much; never having loved much, one will not grieve much; never having given much, one will not receive much; never having befriended much, one will not be deceived much; never having believed much, one will not be disappointed much; but then, one will not have lived much either. Even worse, one will not have been blessed, because one will not have met the living God.

Events moved quickly in our lives to bring us once again to the cross; in fact, we had made our way there without realizing it. In the summer of 1978, for the first time since engineering days, we took a first-class vacation. We went to Bermuda. Before then we had spent our summers camping and driving across the country. Camping had taught me a great deal about handling life's surprises. By enduring bad weather, outhouses, burned and soggy meals, and leaky tents, I discovered the power of anticipatory thinking. When you're camping, you expect misfortune. You see it as part of the script, as inevitable as maps, Coleman stoves, and tent flies.

Is it possible we can handle things better if we know what's coming? Often the things that upset us the most are unexpected happenings. When we plan for peace and quiet and suddenly the telephone rings, the dog attacks the meter man, and the kids start a fight—*then* we lose our cool. If you carry this to its inevitable conclusion, you might call it the power of pessimistic thinking. If you never expect anything to go right, and by some miracle it does, then you can doubly enjoy your good fortune. Perhaps this is why good Calvinists, who expect so little amid the miseries of the world, get along so well. Life's little pleasantries give them unexpected rewards.

Of course, all of this is ridiculous; no one can live with a thorough-going crepe-hanger. Perhaps the answer is cautious optimism—not light-hearted assurance but a confident resolution about the future. In any case, neither of us had planned for what happened when we returned from our vacation in Bermuda that summer.

Joey had been working part-time in an *Abraham and Straus* store for a year. She enjoyed people. She liked selling, and the many friends she had made were good to her. For a few months pains had occasionally flashed through her chest, but she hadn't taken them seriously enough to see a doctor until one beautiful day shortly after our return from vacation. Just as everything seemed very normal and wonderful, the pains suddenly became unbearable. An ambulance took her to the emergency room from the store. Those chest pains saved her life.

The immediate diagnosis was heart problems. The

usual EKGs, heart monitors, nitro-patches, X-rays, and blood tests ensued. Talk of heart catheterization and by-pass surgery began. But something else had been discovered. A spot, or shadow (which is another elusive term for it), appeared in the X-ray on her right lung. More tests began: lung scans, bronchoscopy examinations, tomographs; the probing, the exploring, and the gathering of data seemed endless.

As you submit to the seemingly unending tests, you begin to feel the terror of loneliness and the fear of losing one's identity to a machine. A wondrous eye cuts through bone and tissue, examining the inner workings of the body. Wordlessly it probes. No mercy here. Even the X-ray technicians run for cover behind screens and windows as if fearing the verdict, leaving the victim alone with apprehensions and silent solicitations. The results reveal themselves in pictures, read-outs, and charts. The machine holds the future in its diodes and capacitors, spelling out what's ahead in a special esoteric language.

Life is reduced to procedures and things: the cool hard table of the X-ray machine; the wordless scan of nuclear homing devices; the stainless steel, ceramic tile, and linoleum of the examining room. What happened to color? Warmth? Soft lights? Music? All the things that add life and comfort and peace to our surroundings? Even the art in the hallways is technical, abstract, cubist. Finally, it seems, we are at the mercy of a computer.

The decision came. There was a tumor on the upper lobe of the right lung. In Joey's room, the doctor spoke to us in guarded phrases about matters of life and death. Isn't it strange that topics of such gravity and significance can be discussed with no privacy? Hospitals provide no counseling accommodations. The most devastating matters are whispered in corridors and in rooms, with the television going and the roommate laughing with visitors. With no opportunity to collect ourselves or to talk carefully and tenderly together, we prepared ourselves as well as we could.

Everyone I could think of who knew anything about prayer, I asked to pray. I called every Christian friend I had across the country. I asked at our denominational meeting for prayers for Joey, although in the fifteen years I had been involved in these affairs, I had never heard anyone ask for prayer. I wanted praying people—people who took prayer seriously, not reducing it to sympathy or a get-well card or a fleeting thought over a neighbor's cup of coffee. One person I asked to pray said, "You can count on it. I will put your wife's name on my list for the next two weeks and pray for her daily." Marvelous. When someone asks us to pray for them, we ought to take time to *do* the praying. God hears the fleeting, momentary prayers too, but I believe Jesus learned about his father most in long hours of submission. I wanted people who knew something of those hours and were willing to include my wife's tumor in their relationship with God.

The day of the surgery arrived; it was scheduled for four o'clock in the afternoon. I spent as much time as possible with Joey. We talked about our kids, our vacations, the mountains, and the sea. We kept hearing an ad on the radio for the Russian Tea Room, "Just to the left of Carnegie Hall," and we made a date to go there after the operation. We read Paul, who talked of a God who loved him with a love that X-ray machines, tumors, lung scans—the things that were happening to us now *and* things yet to happen to us—could not defeat. We read and repeated the psalms together. We held hands and found in those moments a sublime trust in God.

They came with pre-op shots. I followed her stretcher to the operating room. I kissed her. She looked at me and said, "shalom," as the pneumatic opener swung the doors apart; then she disappeared into the hospital's most sacred shrine, the surgical unit. At that moment I had no premonitions one way or the other, but as I stood there, hearing the doors hiss shut, I felt confident about God. I felt Paul was right: whatever "things to come" might be, "nothing would separate us from the love of God in Christ Jesus our Lord"(Romans 8:38,39).

I drove home slowly. The surgeon promised to call me from the operating room. She would go directly to intensive care from surgery and stay there a few days. My three daughters prepared supper. We went though the routine of eating. After supper we held hands around the kitchen table and prayed and cried.

The doctor called four hours after I left her at the operating-room door. He said he removed the upper lobe of her right lung where the tumor seemed to be contained. He couldn't say for sure, but it looked malignant. Pathology would have to decide. He took samples of lymph nodes, and though everything else looked normal, he would have to wait for laboratory results. I thanked him and praised God that it seemed contained. I visited her briefly that night and again in the morning. I couldn't believe the progress she had made; I found her sitting up the next day with tubes sticking out of her chest, hooked up to a suction device that sounded like a coffee percolator. I felt encouraged.

I don't believe in signs. I've heard some people get carried away with omens, premonitions, and signals. We once knew a lady who persisted in reading everything from license plate numbers to social security cards. For her they foretold what brand of cereal to buy, what church to go to. In spite of this kind of foolishness, once in awhile something happens that is so startling and timely that you can't help receiving from it an impulsive thought or feeling.

The day after the surgery I drove into the parsonage yard and discovered a lily in full bloom by the porch step. I remembered planting it there at Joey's insistence. I never had much luck with hothouse plants, even if they did say they were hardy. This one had been in our church the previous Easter Sunday. Now in November it burst into full bloom on the most difficult day in our lives.

What gift had we been given? What light shone in the darkness? What hope now seemed confirmed? I quietly praised God for the miracle it seemed to represent and had itself become: Easter in November. It represented resurrection to life. That lily's radiant bloom meant reprieve from malignancy, scalpel, and lab test to rebirth, healing, tea rooms, cormorants, picnics by mountain streams, and most of all praise and gratefulness for the grand miracle of life. I ran into the house to get my Polaroid camera and immediately showed the picture to Joey as a living illustration of hope. We still have that photograph on our wall in the kitchen where it reminds us of God's marvelous grace.

The pathology confirmed the tumor to be malignant; yet no other cancer appeared anywhere. The doctor was cautiously optimistic. *He* said she was lucky, the only person he knew whose life had been saved by a heart attack. *I* said, by the grace of God we live. Like that telegram informing me of the cancellation of my project, this near tragedy reminded me that truth is in the eye of the beholder. No chemotherapy or radiation was recommended. She recovered beautifully from the surgery. As I write this it is a year and a half since she passed through the doors to the operating room, and she remains free of cancer. We praise God and pray daily for her health.

Through Joey's sickness, we discovered new truths about our life and our beliefs.

I remember a fine Christian woman, a long time ago, who became seriously ill. She complained to me of being afraid, especially in the night. She said she was O.K. most of the time, but there were moments of intense fear when demons moved in on her and she trembled on her pillow. She almost seemed to be apologizing to me for being afraid. We talked together about dread and terror. God knows our fear, and we especially need to get over the idea that fear cancels out faith. Fear is not the opposite of faith. The fact is, fear is necessary if faith is to be alive, active, and praiseworthy. We cannot have faith without fear. Faith is dependent on the moments when we feel separated and alone; otherwise our faith would become reality. Faith would be certainty. Could Jesus have been the Christ without the wilderness experience, without temptations, without sorrow, without tears, without Gethsemane, without Calvary?

Fear and faith are at the heart of the classic argument about Jesus. Did he really experience temptation and sorrow and tears *as* temptation and sorrow and tears? In other words was he God? If he was God, then he had the power within himself to easily overcome his troubles without inner struggle. After all, you can't tempt God to tears and sorrow. But if Jesus was man, then part of his battle of manhood had to do with the enticement of self-righteousness; of sorrow that penetrated his consciousness so that he felt grief and self-pity; of tears that produced a sense of separation and despair. As a man, he shared in all that men struggle against and brought to our attention an incredible victory; a victory so complete that we say he managed to remain sinless; a victory so exceptional that we see the very qualities of God in him. As we reflect on our own failures, we see a victory so awesome we hallow the Man who won something much more meaningful than if it were God alone who won. No wonder we make the paradoxical claim for him, "fully God, fully Man."

If faith is to have any sinew and flesh and blood, the faithful need to know something of the struggle to remain faithful. Faith is not magic. It is not as if, once you have faith, the demons go elsewhere to find their victims. No, quite the opposite—the greater the faith, the greater the forces that line themselves against that faith. Look at the principalities and powers that resisted Jesus and finally nailed him to the cross.

When faithful people face darkness and intense sorrow and fear, that is not the time to tell them to have faith, implying their faith is not sufficient or that somehow they have lost it or that they are inadequate before God because of fear. After all, who is adequate before God? In times of intense struggle and separation, it is better to cling to one another and hold hands, understanding the inner ferment that stirs and shakes the soul. And if anything need be said, agree that the experience of terror is breath-taking and debilitating. We learned that we need to allow one another to have fears and that no one should assume faith is lost because of fear. Fear is not a sign of lostness; it is a sign of separation, a valid and essential part of our condition as the faithful.

But another darkness around which we began to see light emerging was the ancient problem of the suffering righteous. The inquiry that recurs in the Old Testament seemed to surround our troubles too: Why do the righteous suffer while the wicked seem to prosper or, at least, escape the pain? Job asked, "Why do the wicked live on, growing old and increasing in power?"[31] Over and over again the question that echoes throughout history is "Where is the God of justice?"[32]

We confront here something that is very difficult to speak or write about. First of all, the trouble lies precisely in the failure of explanations, like the inadequacy of offering a suddenly bereaved widow a medical treatise on heart attacks. Also, religion tends to offer answers that sound overly simple, border on insensitivity, and fail to understand the real terror or pain or separation—which Christianity, of all religions, has the least excuse doing since it has the cross at its heart.

Part of the difficulty is the pain itself. Pain will never be explainable or rational or just, not while such things as nursing homes, insane asylums, retarded children, and lingering, humiliating illnesses exist. Pain is especially irrational to the one who endures it. Pain will not listen to reason.

But if pain is irrational, then so is faith. Was it rational for Abraham to leave the comforts of Ur or for Moses to question Pharaoh or for Jeremiah to criticize Judah or for Paul to write words of triumph just when events seemed ready to destroy him or for Christ to die?

Is it rational to want God in your life? What if he shocks
you out of your complacency, or, worse, begins to shake
up the fragile relationships you manage to live with?
Who needs God to disrupt our private little comforts and
schemes and manipulations? Faith is unexplainable, too.
But the truth emerges that any answer to the discriminate
irrationality of pain is impossible without it. And it is
only from the point of view of faith that any light
emerges upon the question of justice.

With tenderness, humility, and wonder, then, I dare
to say that in spite of the pain this cancer brought into
our lives and in spite of the fear that it might separate us,
we never believed we had been treated unfairly by God.
As I write this now I wonder how we could have been so
accepting of the darkness. All I can say is that it is one of
the mysteries of faith that kept us from despairing over
God's justice. But faith became Presence. Somehow a
great gift of love descended upon us. We clung to each
other believing that while dark dreams invaded us at
night, we had seen enough light to assure us of God's
care. A confidence, trust, and righteousness grew and
nourished us deep within—even to the point that we
praised God for being surely blessed.

Even as Joey's stretcher entered the operating room
we quietly, without expressing it, rejoiced because we
knew the Lord. And like Job we forgot all the complaints
and objections we had stored up to tell him if we were
ever given the chance to do so. During those days all our
questions vanished, and we became intensely aware that
we were not the ones to ask about justice. If anyone
should shake their fists at heaven, it ought to be those
who have not been given eyes to see, who face tragedy

without insight, who lack an organ by which they can perceive God, who die in their sins.

We all at sometime or another seek the ultimate experience of life. We travel to the mountains and to the shores by the sea. We study in universities for truth, searching for something to convict us and capture us. We plan our experiences, and contrive to find gaiety and freedom from our clumsiness and inferiority at parties, on the golf tee, in the club house, and on the tennis court. We sometimes try to turn on more artificially with booze, grass, and chemical trips. Usually, we spend our lives routinely savoring that mythical day of success when our hunger will be satisfied, our pain relieved, our innocence confirmed; but all along we fail to understand that hunger is a gift, pain is power, and innocence is a fantasy. God has the capacity to gather up all the things we count as nothing—those things we yearn to escape from—and through them he becomes a Presence for one grand and glorious moment that makes all other moments, at the same time, inferior and worthwhile.

In those troubled days we learned to cherish the ordinary moments most of all. We caught the uniqueness of this breakfast together on a sunlit porch. We sensed that this task, which we were so often bored with or even loathed, was a gift with possibilities we had not yet seen. We saw pain and culpability a necessary part of the plan. We appreciated over and over again the ordinariness of life. We wondered at the many prayers said for us and saw in vivid color the power they brought to us. We knew ourselves to be blessed. We had wandered into holy places and had been given gifts beyond our wildest dreams. And our cup overflowed.

For it is by grace you have been
saved, through faith—and this not
from yourselves, it is the gift of
God—not by works, so that no one
can boast.

EPHESIANS 2:8, 9

11

The Character of Grace

We reminisced after supper in one of those priceless
times of tears and laughter that are never planned but
simply happen. We talked of the delightful moments we
had shared as a family when we camped across the
country: Mount Rainier in the moonlight as seen from
our sleeping bags; a picnic in a meadow of wild flowers
in Glacier National Park, not a soul within ten miles; a
birthday party on a rainy day in Canada celebrated under
a tarp, with cold lobster and wine, my daughter singing
and playing her guitar, and our sense of well being and
spiritual warmth defying the damp cold all around us.

Then too, we all laughed as we recalled hiking for
three hours across snow and ice to get to a remote,
abandoned fire station in the Tetons. After ascending the

seemingly endless steps to the tower, we were greeted by the most oppressive odor of canned sardines in the closed, sweaty, sun-baked room atop a paradise of mountain vistas. We remembered how much more quickly and unhappily we descended the rickety steps, leaving the two hikers who had arrived before us to their meal and smells and view.

Our children, catching the drift of conversation, began to make much of all the episodes that exposed my short temper. They rapidly recalled incidents when I had lost patience. Suddenly finding myself the victim, I asked, "Thirty years from now as you sit around the table with your children, what will you tell them about me?" Almost in a chorus they said they would remember my restless fuming and fire.

I was shocked; I didn't want to be remembered that way. I wanted them to remember my faith and what God had done in my life and the changes that had taken place because of God, not my aberrations, blunders, and failings. My life had been intercepted by Christ—that alone is worthy of remembrance and praise. I wanted them to see through all the episodes of temper and all my faults to the proof that there is enough light to overcome any person's darkness.

In part, the purpose of this book rests in the desire that my family might see that, as Robert Raines has said, "It was not that I trusted God so much, but that God trusted me."[33] I hope they will catch sight of the immense, enigmatic, unexplainable mercy of God who sometimes picks the most unlikely prospects to work in the vineyard. I pray that God's grace will become apparent as it overflows upon them with the immeasurable glory that remains his alone. As I wrestle with my precarious disposition, perhaps they will know by my errors just how much God has done in my life and see that any virtue of mine is not natural to me. Rather it has been learned as God has trained me for the Kingdom. By God's grace I stumble like a child from light to light, deed to deed, faith to faith.

The Christian good news is, more than anything else, the absurd notion that righteousness has nothing to do with how good you are. It has everything to do with the gift we are given—Jesus Christ our Lord. Incredibly, we are righteous because of Christ, not because of our purity. And that's good news indeed. "Whew, you mean nothing I've done can keep me from righteousness?"

Can you imagine the risks God takes with us? The miracle of grace given to unworthy people is like a thousand-year-old Ming vase given to a drunk as he makes his way across a frozen pond. Yet God calls us his own with all our pimples and blemishes, all our inconsiderate little selfish acts, and all our neglects that we cover up with the petty excuses of fatigue, shortage of time, and more important things to do. And still he persists in claiming, in his own peculiar way, that we belong to him in spite of how ridiculous we make him look. In fact, to our utter amazement, we find ourselves robed and clothed like princes and princesses; we are set before a table of such abundance that we hardly comprehend it—more abundance than we could possibly consume. As part of the King's company, we are included in his most intimate councils, and we are even given a share in his authority and power. No wonder we sometimes feel uncomfortable in such a gathering.

We *know* we will not live up to our billing even if he

doesn't know. We feel as if it won't be long before someone will discover who we really are and then question the King's ability to judge character. People will see we do not belong in such respected company, anymore than someone wearing tennis shoes or socks that do not match belongs at the most important social gathering of the year. No wonder we are sometimes closet Christians. We continue to go along with the crowd and hide our feeble, sputtering lights under bushels, fearing that if his claim for us be known, we will be forced to live up to his impossible dream.

Yet somehow, just as mysteriously as we are chosen, there emerges a confidence and surety. We gradually become aware of a power from which we cannot escape. We slowly accept the joy and beauty of it in the same way that we sense spring coming on. First, the snow blackened by winter's grime shrinks to patches in the shady spots where it was piled up by the plow. Then comes the realization that daylight continues to supper-time. Then a crocus appears like a bright shot from nowhere, as if some bride had dropped a flower from her bouquet hurrying to her wedding. Then the bird, the leaf, the blossom, and the newly turned earth prepared for the seed come into view. We know we have lived to see the spring, and we will be given a share of its abundance, its renewal, its beauty, and its life. It is then we gradually learn that grace, inclusion, glad acceptance, and the Christian life are all miracles.

It is a dangerous notion that this righteousness could be imposed on unworthy people. It doesn't always stand up to careful or critical examination. Our warts can get us into trouble and give God a bad name. One of the great antagonists of Christians these days is Madeline Murray

O'Hare. Her confrontation with a group of Christians on television revealed how vulnerable the Lord has allowed himself to become, because Madeline understands the nature of grace better than we do. She can touch our dark sides very quickly by the outrageous yet calculated statements she makes. And when we lose patience, get angry, and become hostile to her, then with a smile on her face, calmly sitting back and enjoying every minute of it, she says, "And you call yourself a Christian! See, that proves your religion a sham."

We are vulnerable because Christian goals are greater than we are. And Madeline has built a very profitable business based on that. What Madeline doesn't understand is that the Christian faith is an experience more than it is virtue, and because we have been confronted by a presence, something deep within us has changed for the better. Someone once wrote:

> We are all of us more mystics than we believe or choose to believe . . . we have seen more than we let on, even to ourselves. Through some moment of beauty or pain, some sudden turning of our lives, we catch glimpses at least of what the saints are blinded by; only then, unlike the saints, we tend to go on as though nothing has happened. To go on as though something has happened, even though we are not sure what it was or just where we are supposed to go with it, is to enter the dimension of life that religion is a word for.

I read a news item about a family in West Virginia who took in a stray dog and named him Henry. They placed an ad in the lost-and-found section of the local newspaper, but they were unable to find his owner. After several months they gave him to a cousin who lived four hundred and fifty miles away.

Three weeks later Henry scratched at their door after traveling through rain and snow, across highways and backyards, without much food except what he could scrounge from overflowing garbage pails. Henry had come home again.

My theory is that Henry had found something in that household that had changed his life. Maybe he had been touched by some tenderness he had never known before. Perhaps he had been accepted by laughing children whose smiling faces communicated joy instead of abuse, rejection, and pain. Maybe he had simply discovered love for the first time. But I'm sure Henry had experienced *something* that he simply couldn't live without, and he traveled over four hundred miles to find it once more. Religion at its best is like that—being unable to rest until we find ourselves included in the household of mercy, vindication, and love—forever.

It is just then that God begins to claim our deeds as well as our souls. It is Christ alone who makes me aware of the ills my flesh is heir to. I would never know of my lostness except for grace. But maybe it should not be called grace? Without grace I could have gone on making money, vacationing in Hawaii, boating on Long Island Sound, drinking martinis in ignorant bliss without even a twinge of worry about Calcutta or Harlem or Chad or my own soul.

Annie Dillard tells of a curious Eskimo who was struck with the same thought. He asks the missionary priest, "If I did not know about God and sin, would I go to hell?"

"No," said the priest, "not if you do not know."

"Then why," asked the Eskimo earnestly, "did you tell me?"[34]

"What gift is this?" cry the uninitiated, to which we can only reply that to have lived and never seen the sunlight, nor heard Bach or Vivaldi, nor caught a new idea, nor to have ever fallen in love, nor to have ever seen Jackson hit a home run in the ninth with two out and the bases loaded—that is only a hint of what it would be like to have lived without grace. Jesus said that this grace is like a man who discovers a treasure in a field, covers it up, and sells his tickets to Hawaii, his boat, and his bottle of Beefeaters to buy that field. This treasure becomes the one thing we can't live without, so that like Henry we dodge through traffic, wade across snow drifts, and even go hungry to have it.

Still some might suggest that it would be better not to have dodged and waded and hungered. It would be better to play it safe, keep as much as possible for ourselves, and outsmart the opposition whenever we can. But we simply have too much to lose if we allow ourselves to be convinced that charity begins—and ends—at home. Any plea for us to retrench and tenaciously keep all we've been given becomes unthinkable in the light of grace.

Such short-sighted selfishness would cheapen our lives and make us tight-lipped, shallow personalities. It would rob us of life's greatest adventures because it would keep us secure, safe at home, and to ourselves. It would steal the great satisfactions that sharing, loving, and giving bring to us. It would destroy our best and deepest relationships by keeping us on our guard against others, sheltering us against their pain. It would plunder the very best in us—our God-given capacity to be generous, hopeful, free, and at peace with ourselves and our consciences. It would minimize our faith and make a mockery of the trustworthiness of God because we would grow to count more on ourselves than on him. It would keep us from giving our lives to him, and we would never know the exhilarating contentment of the all-too-brief encounters with the Almighty.

I consider myself spectacularly fortunate. With God, there opens up a new wideness to life like coming to the end of the Lincoln Tunnel. The noise of traffic screaming through your brain and the fumes eating at your throat fall away as you emerge into daylight with room to move, clean air to breathe, and quietness to enjoy again.

But God also enriches the senses. They seem to have a quality, an acuteness, they never had before. You recognize a fleeting glance of fear as someone tells you they need surgery. You hear the sound of silence gradually becoming more enriched with the real presence so that you cannot conceive of living without its daily companionship. You touch again the hand you've touched a hundred times before as you impulsively reach out across the breakfast table, and you are grateful for your years together filled with hardship and joy. You breathe deeply of the woods, the wet pine soaking in the rain, and you remember distant places that have become sacred in your memory because you experienced peace and wholeness for a few brief moments there.

God does many things for us. For me he reveals the unity of creation and faith. I can no longer imagine a dichotomy between science and religion even though, over the years, the role of science has been to oppose faith by unmasking the sources of all the dark mysteries, suspicions, and superstitions that had become part of religion. In this role science has served us well by explaining such unsettling occurrences as lightning and storms, and it has reduced the gods of nature to Indian tales and witch's brew.

But now, quite possibly, our physicists will become more mystical than many religious people. Science is rapidly becoming so much harder to believe than religion, that our clergy may end up being the pragmatists and the scientists the believers. The popular idea that science explains everything has been replaced by the realization that science reveals greater and more complex mysteries than even the best science fiction writers could imagine. For instance, science has given us the concept of antimatter—an idea that has stimulated some scientists to speculate about entire galaxies of antiworlds and antipeople. The theory of black holes has emerged from scientific discovery. These bodies of matter are thought to be so dense that even light cannot escape from their intense gravitational force. Due to extreme conditions within the hole, time and space would be interchanged so that it would be as impossible to stop motion as it would to stop time in our system. Another strange phenomena exists in the subatomic world where there appears something called charmed quarks that represent the unpredictability of matter. Imagine that. All along we thought science depended on and affirmed the predictability of things.

With all these discoveries science dares to assert things that are more fantastic than changing water into wine, bringing dead bodies to life again, and healing crippled people who leap and dance with joy. Of course, as theories change and new discoveries are constantly being made, we must be cautious about drawing conclusions. The incredible nature of our world now seems to be bearing out the truth in Isaiah's words: "As the heavens are higher than the earth, so are my ways higher than your ways and my thoughts than your thoughts."[35] Science has helped us see that the more we discover about creation, the more incredible it becomes. And what else could it be if it is the handiwork of God? God, as the ancient men of faith always claimed, becomes awesome.

The material merges with the spiritual. William G. Pollard, a physicist and believer, writes "Now, it is not in the unknown that we find God, but in the mysterious character of the known."[36] The fact that the physical may be less certain and less predictable than we thought leads to the remarkable idea that after all the controversy the spiritual may turn out to be more believable, stable, concrete, and reliable than the material. The real world isn't as solid as we supposed. Man actually does not live by bread alone. Our faith in material wealth and in the accumulation of things appears misplaced; the lasting qualities of those attributes Jesus urged upon us such as love, goodwill, faith, charity, and humility may very well be the Crazy Glue that holds our world together.

Faith now becomes more attractive because it aligns itself with a Power or Mind or Spirit that is at the source of everything we know. More and more there appears to be a within of things, an indwelling presence. Everything, no matter how vast, no matter how small, participates in his plan and in his being. "Even the very hairs of your head are all numbered,"[37] said Jesus. Science has helped us understand what Jesus meant. God concerns himself with the smallest particles in a marvelously charmed way. So too, he concerns himself with me and you, infinitesimal specks in his universe. Norman Cousins said that the significant thing about the lunar voyage was not that men set foot on the moon but that they set eye upon the earth. On the wall of my study I have a picture of the earth taken from the moon to remind me of how small I am and how big God must be . . . and how incredible is the mystery of his coming to someone like me who is no bigger than the hair on a flea's head at the center of Yankee Stadium.

What beautiful possibilities science opens up for us. This marvelous creation has God everywhere in it, so that the proclamation at Bethlehem suddenly fits into the real scheme of things. God materialized in the flesh. The child in the manger, as someone said, did not follow the star, but the star, the very heavens themselves, followed the child.

Therefore, we listen to the child become man, and we realize that all Jesus' talk about justice, truth, immortality, and the inwardness of life is true. Love will overcome hate. Meekness will outlive might. The merciful will obtain consolation. Good overwhelms evil. And all those spiritual things we do, sometimes with tongue in cheek or out of a sense of duty, are not wasted or lost in the vastness of things. All the prayers that sometimes seem so perfunctory are heard. All the little pilgrimages to a lonely old lady in a third-floor apartment in an off-beat corner of the city; all the praise we summon up each day for the bread we eat; all the steaming cups of broth we serve to the sick, the shut-in, and the hungry—all these things enhance his creation and affirm his presence. They become sacrament. We become sacrament—a mixture of spirit and body, as the awesome living God comes within what we call flesh.

And we discover that when we need God in this material existence the most, all the religious things we have done return home to us, lift us, renew us, and reshape us. God invades the material. He claims everything for himself. Everything. Incredibly, undeservedly, even you and me.

Notes

[1] Ephesians 2:4b, 5a.

[2] Augustine, *Confessions* (Harmondsworth, Middlesex, England: Penguin Books, 1961), 21.

[3] Luke 19:5 (RSV).

[4] Charles Fenyvesi, *New York Times*, July 29, 1977, Op-Ed.

[5] Romans 5:3.

[6] 2 Samuel 6:6–11.

[7] 1 Samuel 15:32, 33.

[8] Acts 5:1–11.

[9] C.S. Lewis, *George MacDonald, An Anthology* (Garden City, N.Y.: Macmillan Co., 1962), 85.

[10] Ibid.

[11] Thomas Merton, *The Seven Storey Mountain* (New York: Doubleday and Co., Image Books, 1970), 265.

[12] Aleksander Solzhenitsyn, *The Gulag Archipelago* (New York: Harper & Row, 1974), 168.

[13] Matthew 26:6–13.

[14] Mark 11:22–23.

[15] Luke 19:41.

[16] Luke 22:42–44.

[17] Merton, *The Seven Storey Mountain*, 288.

[18] John Le Carre, *The Spy Who Came In from the Cold* (New York: Bantam Books, 1972).

[19] Aldous Huxley, *Brave New World* (New York: Harper & Row, 1946), 285–86.

[20] Acts 17:22–23.

[21] John 20:24–29.

[22] 1 John 1:1–4.

[23] Lewis, *George MacDonald, An Anthology*, p. 137.

[24] Alistair Cooke, *Six Men* (New York: Alfred A. Knopf, Inc., 1977), 141–42.

[25] Paul Sherer, *Love Is a Spendthrift* (New York: Bantam Books, 1961), 38.

[26] Brother Lawrence, *The Practice of the Presence of God*, (Old Tappan, N.J.: Fleming H. Revell Co., Spire Books, 1977).

[27] Thomas à Kempis, *Of the Imitation of Christ*, (Old Tappan, N.J.: Fleming H. Revell Co., 1963). William Johnson, ed., *The Cloud of Unknowing*, (New York: Doubleday and Co., Image Books, 1973). R.M. French, trans., *The Way of a Pilgrim*, (New York: Random House, Ballantine Books, 1974). St. Francis De Sales, *Introduction to the Devout Life*, (New York: Harper & Brothers, 1950). Elizabeth O'Connor, *Search for Silence*, (Waco, Texas: Word Books, 1972).

[28] Brother Lawrence, *The Practice of the Presence of God*, 12.

[29] Ibid., 37.

[30] Romans 8:26.

[31] Job 21:7.

[32] Malachi 2:17.

[33] Robert Raines, *Going Home*, (New York: Harper & Row, 1979), 41.

[34] Annie Dillard, *Pilgrim at Tinker Creek*, (New York: Bantam Books, 1974), 124.

[35] Isaiah 55:9.

[36] William G. Pollard, *Science and Faith—Twin Mysteries*, (New York: The Seabury Press, 1972), 26.

[37] Matthew 10:30.